SENECA: THE TRAGEDIES

Complete Roman Drama in Translation

David R. Slavitt and Palmer Bovie, Series Editors

SENECA:
THE TRAGEDIES
Volume I

EDITED AND TRANSLATED BY

DAVID R. SLAVITT

THE JOHNS HOPKINS UNIVERSITY PRESS
Baltimore and London

To John Herington, teacher and friend

© 1992 The Johns Hopkins University Press
All rights reserved. Published 1992
Printed in the United States of America on acid-free paper
9 8 7 6 5 4 3

The Johns Hopkins University Press
2715 North Charles Street
Baltimore, Maryland 21218-4363
www.press.jhu.edu

Library of Congress Cataloging-in-Publication Data

Seneca, Lucius Annaeus, 4 B.C.–65 A.D.
    [Plays. Selections. English]
    Seneca, the tragedies / translated by David R. Slavitt.
        p.   cm. — (Complete Roman drama in translation)
    Contents: v. 1. Trojan women—Thyestes—Phaedra—Medea—Agamemnon.
    ISBN 0-8018-4308-1 (alk. paper). — ISBN 0-8018-4309-X (pbk.)
    1. Seneca, Lucius Annaeus, ca. 4 B.C.–65 A.D.—Translations into English.
2. Latin drama (Tragedy)—Translations into English.   3. Mythology, Classical—
Drama.   I. Slavitt, David R., 1935–   . II. Title.   III. Series.
PA6666.A1   1992a
882´.01—dc20   91-36347

A catalog record for this book is available from the British Library.

CONTENTS

PREFACE

We can all agree, perhaps too easily, that bombast is bad. Sanity and proportion are better than madness and exorbitance, and therefore Seneca, being bombastic, exorbitant, and extravagant if not actually crazy, may be dismissed.

This is, more or less, the official position. Seneca has been attacked and vilified, and even his defenders tend to apologize for him, trying to make excuses that he wasn't Aeschylus. We may allow that there is something entertaining about such antagonism, and even that it is convenient to be thus excused from having to attend to a considerable body of work which demands either fluency in Latin or, what may be rarer, the patience to plod through one or another of its unsatisfactory renditions into English. We live in a busy time with many distractions and pressures, and it is a relief to be told that we may skip these plays.

It would be difficult to take issue with that conventional judgment about Seneca's work, except that much of life is disproportionate, extravagant, absurd, melodramatic, and terrifying. Consequently, for an honest artist confronting the irrationality and cruelty of the world, there may be—or even should be—some indication in the art of the stress of that encounter. The classical order and proportion of Greek statuary informs and dramatizes the twists and energy of the baroque carvings. The fiery flowers and landscapes of Van Gogh shimmer with an energy that derives at least in part from his longing for the calm and solace that country scenes are usually supposed to offer.

These plays of Seneca's assume that we are familiar with the earlier versions, the nobler and more restrained broodings of Aeschylus, Sophocles, and Euripides. Seneca is more often than not playing against these models, offering us terrible parodies, even travesties, but with a horrific rather than satiric intention. At the least, we may confidently suppose that the differences in style and attack were carefully considered. This is not the work of a naïf or *primitif*. Seneca, after all, was the son of a prominent rhetorician and was himself an even more eminent philosopher, statesman, and tutor (then minister, and finally victim) of Nero. These are deliberate gestures of an acutely self-aware poet and playwright, and if they are defiantly grotesque, it seems inescapable that the testimony of an experienced man of affairs of a notoriously complicated time deserves at least some notice on the part of serious readers of another era that is every bit as complicated and probably even more cruel. What is the worth of a human life? However we answer—great or middling or small—how can we live with the consequences of what we have said and its implied commentary about the sordidness of the world around us?

The Senecan strategy is not merely an artistic but a philosophic one, the commentary of a man of intimate knowledge of the imperial experience about the ways in which we may withstand life's outrages and disasters. What T. S. Eliot alluded to in his slightly prissy way, in his essay of 1927 on "Seneca in Elizabethan Translation," was "the influence of Seneca upon the 'thought' of the Elizabethans, or more exactly, upon their attitude toward life so far as it can be formulated in words." He went on to elaborate his meaning, suggesting that "Seneca's influence upon dramatic form, upon versification and language, upon sensibility, and upon thought, must in the end be all estimated together." And he arrived, finally, at an elegant formulation in which he asserted grandly and simply that "when an Elizabethan hero or villain dies, he usually dies in the odor of Seneca."

To our shame, it must be said that Senecan deaths are peculiarly contemporary in feeling. There is not merely death but disgrace, violation, sacrilege, even—as in *Phaedra* or *Thyestes*—dismemberment. The intention includes but also goes beyond the dramatic shock of the incident to make a plausible assertion about the vileness of the world. There are two questions that the tragedies of Seneca generally pose, often but not always explicitly. They ask, first, whether there is any divine justice. Are there any gods, or, more particularly, does their mere existence matter to us if they do not occupy themselves with rewarding virtue and punishing wickedness? And then, as a corollary question, Seneca's plays test our assumptions about the limits of the cruelty men and women can visit upon one another. Or worse, he asks whether there are any such limits.

Once these two questions have been posed and answered resoundingly in the negative, the curtain comes down (or, actually, in a Roman theater, goes up). The pity and terror Aristotle taught us to expect from tragedy arise in abundance from Seneca's vivid and passionate demonstrations that we live in a morally indifferent universe and are as bereft and helpless as the figures on stage whose extravagant destructions we have just witnessed. The Aristotelian paradigm, assuming as it does that such disaster comes only to a tragic hero, is more comfortable for us, because of the distance between ourselves and that heroic stature. Unless we are megalomaniacs, we can rely on our insignificance and hope to be spared the attention of the gods, the fates, and such other higher powers as are implied in that world view. In Seneca's plays, the protagonist is often shown to have those very qualities we are ashamed of in ourselves—vindictiveness, implacable spitefulness, and a self-indulgence that displays itself in style and action, producing those typically Senecan tirades. There may or may not be divine powers, but there are surely ghosts, summoned up for their ghastliness and also to supply requisite information about the plot, but there is only occasional reliance upon supernature as the source of human torment. The defects of mankind are generally sufficient to account for any degree of cruelty and suffering. Seneca's is a random and therefore disorderly universe that offers no safe refuge, not even in obscurity. The wretchedness and meanness of the world is everywhere around us, and at the heart of our experience. Indeed, in these plays, the representation of truth is one of deterioration, in which the pattern of dramatic development is a downward and tightening spiral of pain and anger. It cannot get any worse than this, we think, but it does, and then, again, gets even worse than that, until, at the end, we hit bottom, where, along with the agony, there is also a kind of relief that comes from the consoling thud of bedrock certitude.

Lucius Annaeus Seneca was born in Cordoba, Spain, around 4 B.C.

His father, Seneca the Elder, was the well-known rhetorician, and his mother, Helvia, was a woman of considerable intellectual accomplishment. Seneca's elder brother Novatus, who was later adopted by the orator Junius Gallio and took his name, became a politician, and was made proconsul of the province of Achaia (Greece). It was before him that the Jews of Corinth attempted to bring Paul to trial. A younger brother, Mela, is remembered as the father of Lucan (Marcus Annaeus Lucanus), the poet who is best known for the *Pharsalia*.

As an infant, Seneca was brought to Rome and trained in *grammatica* (which is a term that embraces everything from the alphabet through literary criticism), rhetoric, and philosophy. He is said to have been a sickly and delicate child, which may suggest that he was indulged if not actually spoiled. With scanty evidence, one ought to tread carefully, but it seems at least a plausible notion that some degree of cosseting in his youth may have aroused certain optimistic expectations on the part of the young man about a benevolent universe that any ordinary career was likely to disappoint and that service in imperial Rome was sure to have dashed. The gods, after all, are surrogates for our parents, if it is not the other way around. There is an almost theological rage that energizes many of the extravagant scenes and speeches of these plays. Seneca's anger is not merely that of a shrewd and cynical observer but may perhaps be taken as testimony to the wreck of an idealist's faith. Seneca was, at any rate, a follower of Pythagorean doctrines and, for a time, maintained a vegetarian regimen—until his father decided that this was no longer a politically safe or prudent way to live. (Tiberius at this moment was persecuting Jews and certain Egyptians who abstained from pork, camel, and other meats.)

It has been suggested that the study of rhetoric in this period was a peculiarly useless and elaborate pursuit. The formal teaching of rhetoric had been introduced a century or so earlier in a development that had met with some resistance on the ground that the spread of eloquence was likely to result in a spread—and dilution— of privilege. Now that the debates in the courts and the Senate were all but pointless, the functions of these bodies being merely to ratify the wishes and whims of the emperor, oratorical skill was less useful, merely decorative, and therefore more widely admired. Ovid and

Seneca are the two Roman poets who were the main beneficiaries of this hothouse training, or at least whose audiences were likely to admire elegant formulations and tolerate a degree of linguistic self-indulgence and preening.

Because of his frail health—he probably had tuberculosis—Seneca was sent, as a young man, to benefit from the mild climate of Egypt, where his maternal aunt happened to be the wife of the governor. Evidently, his health was restored there and, in 31, he returned to Rome where, with continuing help from this same influential aunt, he managed to become questor in 33 and then, when that term of office was completed, a senator.

In 37, Tiberius died and Germanicus' youngest son, the twenty-five-year-old Gaius—whose pet name was Caligula—succeeded as *princeps*. After Tiberius, it was believed that any change would have to be for the better. According to Philo, Caligula was greeted as a savior who would restore order and reason to the empire. After seven months, however, Caligula was taken ill, and, still according to Philo, the empire fell ill also, but its debility was spiritual, inasmuch as its hopes were stricken: "People recalled how many and terrible were the evils arising from anarchy: famine, war, the destruction of the forests, the devastation of the countryside, and loss of freedom, the fear of conquest, slavery, and death, evils no doctor can cure and which could be treated only by one drug—the recovery of Gaius."

Suetonius tells us that there was such concern, even such panic, as to prompt certain Roman citizens to offer to sacrifice their own lives for the sake of the emperor's, a promise that Caligula, upon his recovery, demanded should be fulfilled. It is difficult to determine whether Caligula had been mad before his indisposition or was in some measure crazed as the result of his illness, but there can be no question about the subsequent peculiarity of his behavior. He had himself deified, and his sister Drusilla, too, whom he married. As a god, he was entitled to resent the competition of mere mortals in those areas where he supposed himself to be preeminently talented. He was therefore annoyed when he was presiding in the Senate and had to listen to Seneca, who spoke so well as to seem to rival his own divine gifts. According to Dio Cassius, Caligula would have had Seneca put to death except for the suggestion of one of the courtiers that Seneca's consumption would kill him soon enough without any governmental interference.

Having been alerted to the precariousness of his position, Seneca relinquished his career as an advocate and turned instead to literary and philosophical pursuits, which were less likely to attract notice. He managed in this way to outlive Caligula, who was assassinated in A.D. 41. But then Claudius ascended to the throne, and Messalina, his third wife, accused Seneca of an adulterous affair with Julia Livilla, Claudius' niece. As a result, Seneca was banished to Corsica, where he lived for eight years (41 to 49), until Agrippina, Claudius's fourth wife, had him recalled and appointed him as tutor to her twelve-year-old son, Lucius Domitius Ahenobarbus—whom we know as Nero (because Claudius adopted him a year later under the name of Nero Claudius Drusus Germanicus Caesar).

Agrippina's was an offer Seneca was unable to refuse. One may wonder, of course, why Agrippina would have chosen Seneca, but it seems a reasonable enough selection if we allow that he was well known and that his long exile might have served to increase his fame. It is likely that he was on good terms with the family of Germanicus (which included Drusilla, Julia Livilla, and Agrippina). Seneca was a respected figure whose help Agrippina could have used in her campaign to get Nero to succeed Claudius. She also turned to Sextus Afranius Burrus, who had distinguished himself as a military tribune and imperial procurator. Agrippina had Burrus appointed as prefect of the praetorian guard, in which position he could moonlight as Nero's other pedagogue.

After Locusta, Agrippina's poisoner, dispatched Claudius in October 54, Nero was proclaimed the new emperor. The first five years of his reign, the Quinquennium Neronis, were a relatively tranquil and prosperous interval, much of the credit for which goes to those tutors who had now been promoted and were acting as his chief advisors. It must have been an exhilarating assignment, for if Aristotle had been able to instruct his pupil Alexander and thereby exert a beneficent influence upon the history of the entire world, what could these two teachers not make together of an even grander opportunity?

Agrippina, however, had less lofty ambitions and, seeing opportunities of a quite different kind, began to plot to replace Nero and put Britannicus (Claudius's son by Messalina) on the throne. Unencumbered by two such high-minded tutors and advisors, Britannicus might be a more manageable protégé. Nero discovered this plot, however, had Britannicus murdered, and as a result encountered such hostility from Agrippina that he was obliged to order that she be drowned. Somehow she managed to survive this first attempt on her life, but her servants understood that she was out of favor and fled, leaving her alone so it was easier for Nero's second team to gain entry to her house, bludgeon her, and then hack her to death in March 59.

Up to this point, the extravagances of Nero had been mostly personal and sexual. It had been said that he went to bed not with his wife (Octavia, daughter of Claudius and the sister of Britannicus) but with his mother, as well as with young boys and older men—and not just slaves, which would have been less disgraceful, but with the freeborn as well. He is reported to have gone through a mock marriage in which he was the bride. But in civil and public appearances, there had been some show of restraint. For example, Nero had been rather less bloodthirsty in gladiatorial combats than other emperors. From here on, it was the mad Nero, albeit without the anachronistic violin.

When Burrus died in 62—possibly of natural causes, but conveniently enough to have aroused some skepticism—Nero turned away from Seneca, his surviving tutor, and instead listened increasingly to the advice of Ofonius Tigellinus, a rake who was a stable owner and breeder of horses for the circus, and Marcus Salvius Otho, who was more or less the imperial pimp (he was later emperor for a little while). Otho had arranged Nero's affair with Acte, who was for a considerable time the official mistress. Not satisfied with Otho's offerings however, Nero commenced a relationship with Otho's wife, Poppaea, who at first supplanted Acte and then was promoted to Octavia's place. Getting rid of Octavia was not easy, because she was Claudius' daughter, but Nero arranged for servants to testify to her adulteries. Even under torture, many of them were unwilling to bear false witness, but enough were found to enable Nero to complete the divorce proceedings. Twelve days later, Nero married Poppaea, Otho having meanwhile been dispatched to govern remote Lusitania (Portugal).

Seneca at this juncture requested permission to retire, was refused, but nevertheless withdrew from the court and the city to spend his time in seclusion, studying and writing—from 62 to 65, when he was accused of having played some part in the Pisonian Conspiracy, a plot to murder the emperor and transfer power to Gaius Calpurnius Piso. Seneca was ordered to commit suicide and obediently opened his veins. Forbidden to make a will, he announced that he was leaving to his friends his richest possession, "the image of his life."

A number of tentative suggestions arise from this legacy, that image we have of Seneca's life. We may, for instance, contemplate the extravagance of his age. There was a lack of limits with which we are presently all too familiar, having lived through the unimaginable cruelties of tyrants and madmen from Stalin and Hitler down through Bokassa, Idi Amin, Pol Pot, and Saddam Hussein. Seneca lived under such arbitrariness and unbounded savagery all the time, from the reigns of Tiberius and Caligula through those of Claudius and Nero. Even if members of the imperial family were not being officially deified, it would have been inevitable for some smart writer to find in the Greek myths and the tragedies to which they gave rise a striking set of precedents for the incest, matricide and patricide, and endless and relentless violations of all the basic pieties and taboos that seemed the main occupation of those who dwelt in the imperial palace.

If Anouilh could find in the *Antigone* a text about resistance to authority that might, during the Nazi occupation of France, carry some contemporary suggestion, there is no reason to exclude the same kind of possibility in the motives and inspiration of Seneca. There were probably numerous different promptings, all of which came together, ganging up on the writer, and driving him. It seems that the temptation to travesty and to "relevance" combined in a fortunate way with that tendency of early imperial Latin rhetoric to show off, as if it were trying to make up by its elaboration and complexity for its lack of consequence and political or judicial power. The decorative but enfeebled oratory of the Senate and the court gives a particular flavor to the declamations of Seneca and his characters' arguments with the gods (who are, in any case, oppressively inattentive).

Finally, there was the body of moral and philosophical essays Seneca had produced, at least in part for the benefit of the young pupil but surely for the edification and improvement of the city and its society. Those essays, Stoicist or Neo-Stoicist (although, actually, Seneca drew on many other schools of ancient philosophy with admirable impartiality, citing Platonists, Cynics, and even Epicureans wherever he thought their insights were valuable) affirm the value of reason in the face of chaos and disorder. This was an affirmation increasingly difficult to make in the reigns of Caligula, Claudius, and Nero, and there is perhaps an element of self-parody in the declarations of some of the Senecan characters—Thyestes in particular comes to mind—of their Stoicist principles. Seneca's words in Thyestes' mouth are a small but not insignificant part of what he eventually has to eat.

One may even go so far as to suggest that the Aristotelian analysis of tragedy, with its emphasis on "imitation of action," involves a set of assumptions about the orderliness and reasonableness of events in history. The nineteenth-century novel, with its underlying notions about how the good are rewarded whereas the wicked are punished, had a similar built-in bias about destiny. It at least assumed the possibility of sequential narrative that could make some kind of philosophical and ethical sense. Senecan tragedies make no such assumption, and they do not rely upon narrative. For that reason, they have been described as more or less static. And this may be accurate. I think of these pieces not so much as dramas as performed poems—masques, we may say. They are not so much representations of an event as they are elaborations on events that are already well known and from which there is no possible escape. The conspiracy in Seneca's work is between the playwright and the audience and its terms are clear enough: both parties know what happens; the challenge is in how much immediacy and specificity the author can summon up, and how much of that we can stand.

The plays speak well enough for themselves. It would be superfluous, and I hope even redundant, for me to suggest any particular interpretations of these works, for translations are, inevitably, acts of criticism. I have tried in these rather free approximations into English to suggest the energy and the pain of the originals, their linguistic pressure. The Elizabethans recognized their power, as, apparently, did Antonin Artaud. There have always been a small number of scholars and classicists who have delighted in these grim pieces and even recognized their power and peculiar relevance to our iron time. For what it is worth, I cast my vote with them. More to the point, I hope these translations may win for this work some of the sympathy and appreciation I believe it deserves.

My practice has not been to try for a word-for-word or even line-for-line series of equivalents. There is, in the Loeb Library, a reliable trot, conveniently tuneless and of considerable help to those with even a little Latin. What I have tried to do, instead, is to be faithful to the dramatic moments. I attempt to find emotional or rhetorical cruces and to connect these in as graceful a way as I can manage in roughly the same number of lines as Seneca used. I have not concerned myself much with whether these things could be played on a stage—although I think it would be interesting to attempt such a production. My primary goal has been for the speeches and the choral passages to be readable, which is to say, sayable. It may be helpful to think of these as spoken oratorios or, if you prefer, old-fashioned radio plays. With a view to that kind of performance, I have assigned the choral passages to a number of designated choristers, mostly because the tradition of choral recitation has all but disappeared and any attempt to revive it would require an unconscionably and uneconomically long rehearsal time.

Finally, I express my particular gratitude to John Herington, at whose kind suggestion I undertook the task of translating these plays. Professor Herington has been friendly and generous to me in many ways, but never more than in setting before me the work of an author he thought I might find congenial and for whom he has such high regard.

TROJAN WOMEN

(TROADES)

TROJAN WOMEN

CHARACTERS

HECUBA, widow of Priam and one of the captive Trojan women
TALTHYBIUS, a Greek herald
PYRRHUS, son of Achilles and one of the Greek leaders
AGAMEMNON, king of the Greeks
CALCHAS, a Greek priest and prophet
ANDROMACHE, widow of Hector and one of the captive Trojan
    women
SERVANT, an aged attendant of Andromache
ASTYANAX, the young son of Andromache and Hector
ULYSSES, king of Ithaca and one of the Greek leaders
HELEN, wife of Menelaus, king of Sparta, and later of Paris,
    prince of Troy
POLYXENA, daughter of Hecuba and Priam (mute part)
MESSENGER
CHORUS of captive Trojan women
SOLDIERS of Ulysses (mute parts)

SCENE: *The shore of Troy, with the citadel smouldering in the background.*

(HECUBA, *in mourning, addresses the audience.*)

HECUBA: Whoever believes in wealth, power, the state,
    those fragile toys of man's contrivance, whoever
    puts his trust in such things and does not fear

3

the whimsical gods, let him look upon me,
and this, behind me—all that remains of Troy.
Never did we imagine the ground we stood on
could give way, shudder, gape open, and swallow
all we had and were. We supposed that gods
had built the city—Neptune, Apollo, mighty
deities both! We believed ourselves to be safe.   10
Nothing is safe or sure but ruin itself.
We trusted in our allies—the Amazons came
with a virgin horde, and Scythians, half-wild,
but Pergamon is fallen, devastated,
her high walls toppled down into dust.
In houses where men and women laughed and whispered,
there are only tongues of flame still jeering now,
or urging the plundering Greeks to be quick and grab
whatever a man can carry. In billows of black
smoke the sky is obliterated: daylight   20
itself is in mourning. The air is thick with ashes
and a foul smell like that of cooking meat,
except that we know it's human flesh, and gag,
and try to hold our breath. The guttering fires
of rage smoulder in the hearts of Greeks, who rub
cruel red eyes in the acrid air, for belief
is not so easy, even for them. The fortress
down? The ten years' battle over? They snatch
trophies, mementos, proofs still hot in their hands. . . .
O gods! O Priam, dead beneath this rubble!   30
And O Hector. . . . His bloodied corpse is lucky
not to behold our shame! Cassandra's ravings
have all come true, her worst nightmares oozed forth
to infect the waking world. When she lay in my womb,
I dreamt that my long labor would bring forth
a firebrand, and now I fear it was true:
It is not crafty Ulysses', or Diomedes',
or lying Sinon's work you see, but mine,
my fire burning there.
                              Why should you care?
Cities grow old and fall, as men and women   40

age and die. Your lives are full of heartache.
Woe does not improve with age, like wine,
to please the refined palate. How hot are the tears,
how salty, how full of body? But listen, imagine
the terrible death I have seen just now of Priam
at the altar in the citadel. Young Pyrrhus,
Achilles' son, with his left hand held the white
and wispy hair and pulled the head way back,
as you might the head of a lamb or kid, and butchered
the old king with a slash so quick the blade   50
came away dry.
      Do you not weep at that?
Do you not feel distress at the lack of respect,
the violation? They killed him at the altar,
as he honored gods who seem to have no care left
for any of us. And still he lies, unburied,
without any funeral torch unless we count
the city, all ablaze, as his ritual pyre.
  They are casting lots for us now, who shall be slave
to whom, which matron or maid will be assigned
as trophy to what lord. The dead are lucky,   60
not forced to watch this humiliation of those
they loved and died for. One lusts after the wife
of Hector, another of Helenus, or Antenor. . . .
They even want Cassandra. Me, they dread,
a terror to them all.
      Make loud lament.
Let Ida resound with wailing, where the judgment
of Paris began what now is ended here.

(CHORUS *of Trojan women files in*)

FIRST CHORISTER: These bitter years have made us all
 adepts: we do not need instruction.

SECOND CHORISTER: Ten times Ida's crest has whitened   70
   with snow; ten harvests have we made,
   resisting the metaphor of the cutting
   down that cried out in the silence.
   No day did not bring fresh griefs.

THIRD CHORISTER: But nothing like this. Lead us, O queen,
   in lamentation and wails of grief.

HECUBA: Sisters, unbind your hair to spill
   over your sorrowing shoulders, pouring
   like tears into the still-warm dust
   of our despoiled city, and rend   80
   your tunics, tear them to tatters, forgetting
   modesty—what husbands have we
   whose honor we keep? Let's bear our breasts
   the better to feel the blows of woe.
   Only the dead and utterly mad
   are safe from these assaults. Let's weep
   with eyes stinging at what they see,
   outraged that they still see, that images
   such as these register in brains
   that rebel. What began with the death of Hector   90
   goes on, beyond what mortals can bear.

FIRST CHORISTER: We have unbound our hair, have prayed
   at many a funeral, sprinkled our faces
   with ashes, our garments loosened and torn,
   flailed at our bosoms with small fists,
   enraged and impotent. Words are no good.
   And our wordless cries fade on indifferent
   air. The shore resounds, and Echo
   repeats our plaint from the mountain caves,
   but quiets at last. The sea should rage,   100
   and sky should crack with thunder and mother
   earth join us in mourning, beating
   her breast as we beat ours, her palms
   stinging with a consoling pain.

The noise should be louder and greater, as great
as the reason for our moaning—we weep
for the death of Hector, the fall of Troy!
For all time, desolation will take
as its standard this bleak moment. The world's
woes will forever compare themselves   110
to what we suffer here this day.

HECUBA: Blood cries out for blood—the wounds
of Hector's body are all mouths
calling out for a mother's care,
the blood demanding repayment in blood.
I tear my own flesh, lamenting
that nothing I do can bring him back,
nothing I do can wash away
the rage and grief. The blood pours out
as irreversible as the time   120
of a man's life that oozes away,
golden, crimson, then pitch black.
O my son, you were the bulwark
of Troy, its strength, its will, its wall.
Atlas holds up the sky, as you
held on your strong shoulders the city,
and when you fell, it fell, we fell.
Your last day was ours. We mourn
ourselves as we mourn you and Priam.

SECOND CHORISTER: Dare we even speak of the king,   130
of how his body lies unburied
at Jupiter's altar.

THIRD CHORISTER: Hecuba's sons
in their long cortege, and then King Priam!
He lay himself prostrate at the altar
and there became the sacrifice
in a barbarous rite. His body still
is stretched out on the bloody floor—
without the head they severed from it

and took as trophy. Who could imagine,
or knowing that such a thing has happened,   140
comprehend it? Numb, we say
the words and wait for some of the meaning
to sink through into our skulls and hearts.

HECUBA: Do not mourn for happy Priam:
    We are the captives; he is free.
    Never on his neck will the yoke
    of conquerors gall a noble spirit.
    He will not have to bow his head
    to Atreus' sons or crafty Ulysses.
    Those royal hands that held the scepter   150
    will never be fettered. He will not march,
    a slave in Mycenae's vulgar parades.

CHORUS: Let us all say, "Happy Priam!"
    for he has taken his kingdom with him.
    Now in the shades of Elysian Fields
    his spirit wanders with pious souls,
    and he seeks his son the noble Hector.
    Death has come to give him a better
    and gentler end than we may expect.

(*Enter* TALTHYBIUS)

TALTHYBIUS: Another delay! Outward bound or homeward,   160
    the voyages of Greeks seem not to go smoothly.

FIRST CHORISTER: What is the cause of this delay? What checks
    the Greeks now in their homeward progress? Tell us.

TALTHYBIUS: It sounds like a simple, perfectly innocent question,
    but, knowing the answer as I do, I feel
    the terrible vertigo of the deep abyss
    that suddenly opens, turning the solid ground
    perilous. There ought to be portents, earthquakes,
    waterspouts, an eclipse, volcanic eruptions

with huge boulders that fall from the sky, but nothing   170
obtrudes upon the day. The sun still shines,
in mockery and deception. Birds chirrup
on branches of trees that should be uprooted in floods
that sweep the valleys clear of all habitation.
Catastrophe wants some darker, more dramatic
background than this. It isn't right. I should not
have to speak words that will change not only air,
but earth and sea, and ignite the fire that waits
to consume our substance. Mighty Achilles' spirit
does not sleep easy yet. His famous wrath   180
still simmers and makes the same proud demands
he made in life. You know who his mother is:
Thetis, the sea goddess. She now impedes
our ships in the harbor. We must give way, appease
her darling son and cater to him once more
as we have always done. The word from the priests,
dreadful but perfectly clear, is that he demands
the tribute due his spirit. "I want my share
of the booty, one of the Trojan women. I want
Polyxena," he says. I know, he's dead,   190
but you can't reason with demigods and heroes,
or talk them around. They say some outrageous thing
you think must be a joke, but they insist
no matter what disaster it means. He demands
Polyxena. Sacrificed. His son
Pyrrhus, he has instructed to perform
the bloody rite, and scatter the poor girl's ashes
upon his grave. The winds and waters confirm
the priest's report. The ships won't move—cannot—
until we have carried out these dreadful instructions.   200

(HECUBA and CHORUS are horrified. They watch as PYRRHUS and
AGAMEMNON enter. CHORUS sits and attends to the following scene
as if they were part of the audience.)

PYRRHUS: Pictures of home filled your minds as wind
  was to fill the sails of the ships, bellying out
  in pride. No thought for Achilles, by whose hand
  the victory was achieved. The blow he struck
  left Troy a blasted tree, about to fall
  this way or that, according to which wind
  should happen along. The holds of those ships are full
  of the swag of a conquered city, rightfully his.
  Every chief has his share, but for my father,
  the best of all the Achaeans, no prayer of thanks   210
  to his great spirit, not even a thought. Insulting!
  Your destiny was here, you were compelled;
  but he had a choice, might have preferred a long
  and quiet life, as his mother, Thetis, urged.
  But his noble soul prompted the other way,
  for glory's sake, to seize the occasion, to sign
  history's page with his name. And have we already
  forgotten his prowess, his sacrifice? Was it all
  for nothing? He chose to come, fighting his way
  to get here, battling Mysians, who barred   200
  his passage, and hacked his way through a thicket of dead
  to arrive at this field of honor. What honor now?
  Other heroes' exploits pale in the light
  of what he accomplished even before he arrived
  at this accursèd strand. But what he achieved
  here was more and greater. From Hector alone
  his fame should be secure throughout the ages.
  It ought to be, but isn't. The Greeks, themselves,
  his own companions in battle, have put him aside,
  and he is forgotten. My father conquered the Troy   230
  you have plundered. His glorious deeds of battle
  enrich you all: Hector dead, slain
  in front of his father's brimming eyes; Memnon,
  the demigod, the son of Aurora, dead
  as the bleakest dawn; Penthesilea, queen
  of the Amazon women, dead. My father's worth
  is weighed in a scale that holds those mangled corpses.
  You are so much his debtor that he could ask

a prize from Argos, of your own house and blood—
to spill which, once, you did not hesitate   240
with the wind in another quarter. Iphigenia
you gave up for the cause. And now, having won,
a new humane spirit obtains? We become
considerate? Kind? My father, Achilles, demands
the sacrifice of one of the Trojans merely,
one of King Priam's get! Is Peleus's son
by any measure of fairness to be denied?

AGAMEMNON: The rashness of youth must learn restraint.
    Your age
is passionate, fervent. Any young man would be,
even without Achilles as a father—   250
whose rages I remember well and endured,
as a leader must, intemperate outbursts
of one on whom responsibility weighed
with less oppression. But you do your noble father
an injustice—his pride we all remember,
but there was also mercy. The bitter struggle
taught us all and changed us all. By the end,
he was a kinder man, had learned how victors
ought to behave to the vanquished, how to be moved
even to tears by suffering he had caused.   260
Great power we hold, but only a while:
it comes and goes, as if with a will of its own.
Fortuna raises us up and casts us down
in endless vicissitude—and we should learn
not to be arrogant, and not to be ashamed
at the heights and depths, those matters of great moment
but only at the moment. Fear the gods,
and fear them most when they seem excessively kind.
Do the ruins of Troy make you happy? Strong?
Invincible? A creature of destiny? Think   270
how weak and paltry a thing is man, and quake
that grandeur, wealth, and strength can be overthrown
and turned to the sorry rubble we behold.
I have been guilty of pride, but I was wrong.

Let us learn from Priam the difficult lesson,
that crowns can topple, and skulls beneath are fragile
as those of any men. Ten years, ten seconds,
a thousand ships, or none, and what we believed
to be real, solid, evaporates, is smoke
in the acrid air. I wanted this to happen,   280
I do confess, but now my wrath is spent.
The blood lust has subsided, but Troy cannot
be built again, or all those dead brought back.
But those who have survived, let them alone . . .
Let there be an end of bloodshed, a hope
among mankind of decent pity. You ask
for another innocent victim, a grisly rite
where murder masquerades as a kind of marriage.
Her blood would be on my head and hands and conscience.
But it won't. No, I will not let it happen.   290

PYRRHUS: Shall Achilles' ghost have no reward at all?

AGAMEMNON: Praise, he shall have, and immortal fame. His name
    shall live among men forever! What greater reward
    could anyone want? If there must be blood shed,
    let it be that of the Phrygian cattle, slain
    to do him better honor than bitter tears
    of the mother of some poor girl. For civilized men,
    human sacrifice is . . . absurd and hateful!

PYRRHUS: O brave and noble king! O wise and just . . .
    in good times, and in safety, that is. Your heart   300
    is full of good will, as you romp with your concubine.
    Danger evokes a somewhat different aspect,
    fierce, realistic . . . honest, one might say.
    With this right hand, I shall give my father his due—
    with the same right hand as cut off Priam's head!
    Let it be noted that Pyrrhus is not afraid
    of doing violence to kings.

AGAMEMNON: I do not deny it.
You did, indeed, kill Priam—a glorious deed!
An old, defenseless man who was your father's
suppliant, and you slew him!

PYRRHUS: And am proud 310
so to have done, knowing my father's friends
and suppliants, as I knew his enemies too.
Priam at least, when he had to plead with my father,
was brave enough to come himself. The danger
as well as the chagrin he managed to swallow.
But you, when you had to beg him to fight again
to save the Achaeans, showed less well, or rather
showed not at all. You hid in your tent and sent
others to make your case, Ulysses and Ajax.
You couldn't face him!

AGAMEMNON: A coward, then, do you call me? 320
Had I not struggled in the battle, while your father
lolled on the couch in his tent, strumming his lyre
and singing along?

PYRRHUS: And did not Hector's tune
change when my father came to rejoin the ensemble?

AGAMEMNON: And Priam came at last to that tent to beg!

PYRRHUS: Was it not noble to spare the life of a king?

AGAMEMNON: Then why in the name of the gods did you kill that
king?

PYRRHUS: Death, sometimes, can be a mercy, too.

AGAMEMNON: Is mercy what you want for the Trojan maiden?

PYRRHUS: Has the sacrifice of maidens become a crime 330
suddenly in your book?

AGAMEMNON: Sometimes a king
   must put his country's interest before his children.

PYRRHUS: No law protects these lives: these people are captives.

AGAMEMNON: Shame can forbid sometimes what the law does not.

PYRRHUS: Having the right, we are in the right! What shame?

AGAMEMNON: Having the power, we also should have the
      grace . . .

PYRRHUS: You are spouting nonsense! Ten long years we fought
   with proud, mad Priam—whom I destroyed!

AGAMEMNON: Sir, you go too far!

PYRRHUS: In Atreus' house,
   is there such a thing as going too far?

AGAMEMNON: Take care!   340

PYRRHUS: I am Achilles' son, whose line goes back
   through Thetis and Acacus even to Jove!

AGAMEMNON: Achilles is dead, remember. You are not immortals.

PYRRHUS: But even immortals feared Achilles.

AGAMEMNON: Silence!
   I could correct your manners, but my sword
   knows how to spare captives, and I must do
   no less for my own allies. Let Calchas, the priest,
   decide. If the fates demand it, I will yield.
   (*Enter* CALCHAS)
   You know the secrets of sea and sky. Your art
   can read the waterspouts and shooting stars,   350
   discover their meanings, and bend the will of gods

to accommodate our purpose. Your arcane skills
have cost me dearly, and yet you brought the result
we required then. We need you to riddle again
the illness of the winds and declare a cure.
What is the will of the gods, Calchas? Tell us!

CALCHAS: The voyage may proceed, but the price remains
   dear—what we paid before, we must pay again:
   a maiden's blood. The sacrifice, this time,
   must be on the tomb of Achilles, in the guise   360
   of a marriage rite, as brides are given at home
   in Sparta or Mycenae. Let Pyrrhus lead
   his father's bride to the altar. And this is half!
   To Polyxena's blood must be added even more:
   Priam's grandson, Hector's little boy,
   Astyanax, let him be led to the rampart
   and from the tower flung! Our thousand sails
   will belly then with wind. And this is all!

(AGAMEMNON, PYRRHUS, TALTHYBIUS, *and* CALCHAS *exeunt.*
CHORUS *gets up. They whisper among themselves. Then they speak.*)

FIRST CHORISTER: What is said of the soul, do we dare
   believe? Or disbelieve? Our fears   370
   either way are dire—that flesh
   dies and rots and nothing is left
   is a terrible thing, but the other is worse,
   that our travails could go on forever,
   the pains and rages that flesh can suffer,
   the spirit must suffer forever, yearning
   for the black night we thought we dreaded.

SECOND CHORISTER: A man's breath on the winter air
   is a ghostlike puff, and disappears
   to mingle with other gasses and vapors.   380
   Can all those sunsets, all those dawns
   simply stop and come to nothing?
   Can the riot of stars, the ebb and flow

of tides, the rushing of fate itself
empty into a still pool
of the Styx where nothing ripples or gleams?
Which do we want it to be, and which
ought we to fear? Smoke from a fire
rises to stain the air, but the blackness
erases itself, and the sky is blue.   390

THIRD CHORISTER: In that pellucid air, no ghost's
    shadow darkens the even glare
    of sunlight or the flicker of starlight.
    Nothing remains after a man
    is burnt on the pyre or buried in earth.
    That business of Hades is just a story
    for children we still believe because we
    are children, too, but we know better
    and worse—that Achilles' spirit is merely
    a fiction, as Greeks know perfectly well.   400
    Where do we go, then, after we die?
    To wherever they are who never were born!

(*Enter* ANDROMACHE, *leading her young son,* ASTYANAX, *and accompanied by an aged* SERVANT.)

ANDROMACHE: Why do you weep, women of Troy? Our griefs
    cannot be compassed in wailing and tears. Such signs
    of trivial woes are not for us whose hearts
    are devastated, sacked, and burned. A city
    smoulders in ruins in each of us. My Troy
    fell when Hector fell and that beautiful body
    was dragged along in the dust to make a trench
    I might have filled with tears, but did not, numb   410
    as a tombstone is and dumb. My life is over.
    Having escaped the wilding Greeks, I'd gladly
    follow my husband's shade, were it not for our son
    who needs me, keeps me alive, and, with his love
    prolongs my anguish. Happiness is a dream,
    and the only satisfaction I can imagine

arises from scorn, defiance, the hatred of Greeks—
but I cannot let them guess what I feel, and envy
those stones that have been my teachers and know no fear.
Disaster gapes at our feet. It is bitter indeed   420
when fear has survived the death of every hope.

SERVANT: What is there now to fear? Why this new terror?

ANDROMACHE: It is not finished yet. There is always more
and worse to fear, beyond imagination.

SERVANT: What worse could the gods possibly dream up now?

ANDROMACHE: Only a fool would ask such a question. The caves
of Hell are rich in terrors that wait to rise
through flaws in the earth to infect the lives of men.
What's past is never past, but endures like plague
to taint the air. Old hatreds, jealousies, rages   430
everywhere lurk like vipers, sleeping or only
feigning sleep but ready to strike. Achilles'
restless ghost paces the beach, and Hector's
sorry and inarticulate spirit warns
that nightmare evils will break forth into daylight.

SERVANT: Say what terrible dream prompts this new fear.

ANDROMACHE: I think—I hope—it was a dream. Exhausted,
I lay awake as the distant stars performed
their set routine. I think I fell asleep
or at least into the stupor of a dazed,   440
distracted mind. Who knows what it was? But Hector
seemed to stand before me, not the Hector
I should have liked to summon, fierce and noble,
ready to do battle with Troy's attackers,
slaughter their ranks, kill their savage chieftains,
and even seem for that one, wonderful moment
to have slain the haughty Achilles. This was the other,
worn Hector, as tired as I, and as full

of bitter griefs, but even so, my heart
fluttered to see him again. He shook his head   450
and spoke, in a kind of anguished whisper: "Wife,
rouse yourself from slumber. Save our son!
Hide him away somewhere and keep him safe—
you are his only chance."
                              I could not move,
overcome with emotion. He bade me hurry,
speaking again: "Do you think the fall of Troy
is yet complete? There are further depths to plumb,
even more bitter griefs to endure. Make haste.
Get him away, out of this cursèd house,
and put him where they'll never think to look.   460
Do it, now!" I rose to obey, but thought
to embrace him one last time, to hold my husband
once again in my arms . . . but he was gone,
melted away in the darkness, as ghosts do,
and leaving me widowed a second time and bereft
with freshened loss.
                     My son, remnant, relict
of a stricken if illustrious house—his face
is Hector's, and those same features and carriage
recall, mixing joy and pain, his father's.
A day will come when Astyanax shall avenge   470
Troy's ruin, restore the justice of heaven,
and drive back into the ocean the greedy Greeks.
One day, he shall rebuild those towers and walls . . .
although I hardly allow myself the hope
of seeing it happen. Enough for us poor captives
to live from moment to moment, but for my son,
I hope and therefore fear. . . . Where can I hide him?
The citadel is violated, doors
hacked to bits, each one, for the scraps of treasure
that might repay the effort it took some Greek   480
to break it down. Not even a child could find
a refuge there. What place may escape their notice,
unpromising or even forbidding enough. . . ?
Lord Hector's tomb, that simple structure of hewn

stone, would inspire awe, even from those
vandals. To his father, then, will I send
and entrust the child, although I dread the omen.

SERVANT: You do not have time. Decide quickly, and act!

ANDROMACHE: I fear it's hopeless. Someone will surely betray us.

SERVANT: Then do it all alone.

ANDROMACHE: The Greeks will ask!   490

SERVANT: You'll say he was killed in the fighting. How will they
     know
  it isn't true? Your grief will not be feigned.

ANDROMACHE: It won't work. Nothing we do succeeds.
  We're doomed.

SERVANT: You cannot know that unless you try!
  He's still alive, as you are. There must be hope!

ANDROMACHE: (*To* ASTYANAX) I wish there were some remote
     inaccessible place,
  an unlikely place that would keep you safe. O Hector,
  you were the one we looked to for safety, courage,
  and faith, and only then for strength. What good
  is strength without the faith to use it? Lord,   500
  I come to you once again, unworthy, afraid,
  but doing the best I can. Protect our son.
  Child, enter the tomb. Your father's spirit
  is nothing to fear. Do not shrink back. It's safe!
  Or does that safety shame your noble spirit?
  Be sensible! Acknowledge that we are weak,
  helpless—a captive woman, a little boy.
  We must yield to the force of our misfortune.
  Enter your father's resting place and, if fates
  be kind, your sanctuary. If not, your tomb.   510

(ASTYANAX *enters the tomb, and its gates are closed*)

SERVANT: He will be safe there. Let us withdraw a bit,
  so as not to attract attention to this place.

ANDROMACHE: As if the things we do made any difference. . . .
  But we must make the effort. Let us go.

(*They walk a few steps but see someone approaching and stop*)

SERVANT: (*Sotto voce*) Say nothing. Do not give yourself away
  or him. It's Ulysses, worst of the bad lot.

ANDROMACHE: (*Looks toward the tomb*)
  O earth, I pray you, keep him safe. Hide him,
  cradle him safe, as a mother holds a babe
  close to her bosom, or as you hide bear cubs
  in secret caves when hunters come. This hunter   520
  is tricky and cruel. I fear what he may do.

(ULYSSES *enters with* SOLDIERS)

ULYSSES: Madam, I speak officially. What I say
  is not what I choose but what I am forced to tell you
  as a part of my duty. My words come from the council
  of all the Greeks. Our ships are unable to move,
  and action must be taken. Hector's son
  prevents our embarkation—a state of affairs
  that cannot be permitted. It isn't easy,
  but I must ask you to give him over to us.
  He threatens the peace. His life itself is a danger   530
  we cannot allow to continue to undermine
  the entire region's collective security. Greek
  power and prestige cannot be questioned.
  Ours is a stabilizing presence, and fear
  and hope, by their very nature, destabilize,
  which would mean the end of everything we have fought
  to achieve here. Calchas, the seer, has pronounced

a hard judgment, but one in which all concur.
You know, in your own heart, what we fear is real.
A son grows up to be like his father, and Hector   540
is not a figure we wish to encounter again.
The newborn calf is a pleasant pet, but grows
to become the dangerous bull that rules the meadow,
as strong as his sire. I understand your grief
and, indeed, respect your feelings, but you must see it,
must understand our position, after ten years,
ten long winters here and bloody battles
the like of which have never been seen before.
On both sides we know too well what war is like,
and want not to have to go through it again.   550
This is Calchas's interpretation: the winds
will not change as long as the boy survives.
Dreadful, but that's how it is. Agamemnon's son,
Orestes, would not be allowed to delay our departure.
Iphigenia suffered; I fear it is now
the lot of the vanquished to suffer what the victors
have already had to endure. I am sorry, madam.

ANDROMACHE: I have no idea where he is. I have wept and
        prayed
    to the gods, who alone know whether hostile spears
    have pierced his little breast, or whether he roams   560
    like a lost pup on the desolate fields, or lies
    burned in the ashes of whatever building or shed
    he hoped to hide in. Perhaps some wild beast got him.
    The truth is that I hoped you were bringing news . . .

ULYSSES: Exactly what I expected you would say,
    but it won't work. We'll get the information.
    There's no point drawing it out or playing games.
    Tell me, madam, where is your son hiding!
    Out with it!

ANDROMACHE: Where is Hector? Where is Troy?
    Where is Priam? You look for one small boy,   570
    but I look for a city!

ULYSSES: Sooner or later,
    you know you are going to tell me. Sooner is better.

ANDROMACHE: Is that a threat? Those who wish to die
    have a kind of safety.

ULYSSES: The fact of death is different
    from the very pleasant abstract idea.

ANDROMACHE: Try me!
    Kill me! Do me that favor, and I shall be grateful!

ULYSSES: There are easy deaths and hard ones. Torture is not,
    I am sure, what you have in mind for yourself. In pain
    one's resolution crumbles. The self dissolves,
    and honor and love turn out to be nothing but fictions.   580

ANDROMACHE: Bring on the instruments—the burning tongs
    and all that banal paraphernalia. I dare you,
    discover the depths of my grief and also my hatred!

ULYSSES: Nicely done. But that speech I have heard
    before. It is part of the ritual, nothing more.

ANDROMACHE: Were all those other victims bereaved mothers?

ULYSSES: Defiance will do no good. It only proves
    what I have been saying all along, that Greeks
    are right to fear your son. After this long
    and bitter fighting, there's no other way. We cannot   590
    allow our gentler impulses to condemn
    the world to another war in which Telemachus
    and your son reenact this sorry story.

ANDROMACHE: It won't happen. I tell you I was sure
you came to tell me that Hector's son is dead.
There is no Astyanax to cause the brave
chiefs of the Greek host any nervousness.

ULYSSES: I need some shred of evidence. What have you?

ANDROMACHE: You want a body? Take mine, or take my word,
my solemn oath—that Astyanax, my son,   600
lies with his father's dust, among the dead.

ULYSSES: I am relieved to hear that the peace is secure
and will take this report back to the Greeks.
(*Aside to one of the* SOLDIERS)
                                          They'll laugh,
or else, convinced I've lost my mind, will send
another, saner messenger. What mother
would not swear falsely to save her son? Her oath
however solemn, weighs like other words
that float on the thinnest air. There is always torture,
but that should be the last resort. It's clumsy,
and reflects badly on those who resort to it   610
too quickly. It's also unattractive.
There must be a ruse, some stratagem to wring
the truth from a mother's unwilling lips. She grieves,
that's true enough, but there's no end of weeping
and groaning on this blasted shore. We'll see
whether grief gives way to fears it hopes to hide.
(*To* ANDROMACHE)
My impulse is to offer condolence. To you,
I extend sympathy—also congratulations
for what you and he are spared: a cruel death
awaited your young son. He would have been cast   620
from one of the wall's still standing towers to fall,
even before your eyes, to the rocks below.

ANDROMACHE: (*Aside*) I must not let my terror show. My lip
trembles as if from cold. My knees are water.

ULYSSES: (*Aside*) She trembles, does she? With fear? She betrays
    herself.
  Her oath counts for less and less. . . . We'll see.
  (*To his* SOLDIERS)
  Look for the boy. The mother has hidden the brat.
  This is the last of our hard labors at Troy.
  Go, find him. Bring him at once to me,
  quickly.
  (*He waits for a moment or two as they go off, then calls out*)
        Aha! They have him!
  (*As if calling orders to* SOLDIERS)
                       Drag him here!   630
  (*To* ANDROMACHE, *who looks frightened*)
  But why do you look so terrified? The boy,
  you swore, was dead. Surely, you spoke the truth.

ANDROMACHE: I wish it were a lie. This is my normal
  look, what my face has learned from years of war.

ULYSSES: (*Thinks a moment and looks at Hector's tomb*)
  Madam, I yield. I acknowledge myself defeated.
  We cannot perform the rite Calchas prescribed.
  The ships must nevertheless depart, and the gods
  must be propitiated. Therefore, lacking
  the son, we shall make do instead with the ashes
  of Hector, himself, scatter them to the winds   640
  and pray they favor our westward voyage home.

ANDROMACHE: (*Aside*) He has guessed. He knows, is toying with
    me. . . . Or is it
  only an unlucky coincidence?
  What shall I do? I cannot think! My mind
  doesn't work, but panic and my conviction
  that it's all a matter of ill luck, that nothing I do
  can save my son, prevents any kind of thought
  except to call on the gods, in whose compassion
  I believe no longer. . . . On the contrary, hard
  and cruel and brutal is what they are, and the worst   650

is what's most real. I'd pray to Hector's ghost,
but what should I pray? That they scatter his bones? That,
     instead,
they kill our son? Which should I try to snatch
from their horrid hands? I suffer, as if the choice
were mine to make—in which event, not I
but hatred should make it: the one the Greeks most fear
is the quick Hector, the threat of the new Hector,
for the father is in the son. But how can I save him?
I'm helpless, and the cruel gods use Ulysses
as an instrument with which to torture me.   660

ULYSSES: For the embarkation, then, I will raze the tomb!

ANDROMACHE: Would you take back the body Achilles gave
   to Priam?

ULYSSES: Do not quibble. It will not work.

ANDROMACHE: I shall appeal to Pyrrhus. His father's honor
   ought to count for something!

ULYSSES: (*To his* SOLDIERS)
                              Break down the door!

ANDROMACHE: (*To his* SOLDIERS, *but for* ULYSSES *to overhear*)
   This is a sacrilege. You cannot touch it,
   even you, for whom nothing is holy. Temples
   you have profaned, but up until now our tombs
   your spite has spared. Some primitive reverence flickered
   in the blackness of your hearts. If nothing inhibits   670
   the desecration of graves, I shall, myself,
   oppose you, with bare hands. My passion, hatred,
   disgust will give me strength. An Amazon
   or mad Maenad, I'll tear your eyes with my nails!

ULYSSES: (*To* ANDROMACHE)
  Very impressive. Very moving, indeed!
  (*To* SOLDIERS)
  Ignore her. I have given you my orders.
  Carry them out. This woman's tears and rage
  have nothing to do with you.
  (ANDROMACHE *struggles with* SOLDIERS)

ANDROMACHE: Murder me first!
  Strike with your blades! You cannot do this! Villains!
  Beasts! Vermin! Hector, help me! Heave   680
  your body back to life. Come to my aid
  and teach Ulysses a lesson in decency.
  Even your ghost is stronger than he.
  (*In a sudden calm*)
                                  Lord Hector!
  You come! Your mighty sword is high above
  your helmet's waving crest!

ULYSSES: She's gone quite mad.
  Pay her no mind, I tell you. Open the tomb.

ANDROMACHE: (*Aside, as they get the heavy door open*)
  How can this be happening? The dead
  and living should not be outraged by the same
  foul deed! I cannot even imagine
  a prayer, except that the heavy tomb should collapse   690
  to kill Astyanax and the Greeks together,
  all crushed among Hector's bones! But nothing
  happens. Nothing interrupts. Nothing.
  (*She kneels before* ULYSSES)
  I kneel before you, a suppliant. I touch
  my hand, which no man's foot has ever known,
  to yours, to beg for pity. Misery pleads,
  and what one gives to Misery, Fortuna
  remembers and may one day repay. Think
  of your own dear wife at home, of your own son,
  whom you love and hope one day to see again.   700

For the sake of what you feel for your own, and in common
humanity, common and simple decency, spare me!

ULYSSES: Produce your son. Then pray.

ANDROMACHE: Astyanax,
   come out to your wretched mother. Come.
   (*He appears*)
   Here he is, the one you fear,
   the terror of a thousand ships.
   (*To* ASTYANAX)
   Pray with me to the conquering Greek.
   Ask, as your mother does, for mercy.
   Forget the pride of your father's house.
   To this have the fates brought us, the gods   710
   themselves have burdened us. Lower your head
   to touch the floor. It is no disgrace.
   Weep, as your mother does, and hope
   your tears may soften their hard hearts.
   (*She turns to* ULYSSES)
   Hercules once conquered Troy
   and slew the king, Laomedon,
   but he spared the child, the young Priam,
   and placed him upon his father's throne,
   moved by the child's tears of entreaty.
   If such a hero could be so moved,   720
   you may surely allow yourself
   the promptings of those human feelings
   I assume you have, deep down somewhere.
   What is there, after all, for a soldier
   but glory, now and for all time?
   You could share, could bask in the light
   of the hero of heroes, for gods have contrived
   the same opportunity now for you
   to spare the young heir to the throne
   who lies before you and pleads for his life.   730

ULYSSES: Who could not be moved? I'm human, humane—
   or like to think so—and a mother's grief is moving!
   But I have to think of the mothers of Greece, whose tears
   I would hear one day if I let that boy grow strong
   to take up arms against their little boys.

ANDROMACHE: How can he be a threat? Sir, look around you,
   consider these smouldering ruins, the dust of our city.
   Can he, in a lifetime, rebuild, rearm, revive
   the mighty Troy you conquered? The dead are dead,
   and he has seen them, watched as his own father   740
   was dragged in the dirt. What pride can he have, what lesson
   in courage and honor? Wounded, broken, his spirit
   is nothing to cause you fear, is that of a slave . . .
   which you must recognize. Let him live, in bondage,
   a yoke upon his noble neck. I beg you!

ULYSSES: It is not Ulysses refusing, but rather Calchas.

ANDROMACHE: They say you are clever, crafty. Where is
      your craft
   now? You can surely contrive some plausible story,
   that the boy is dead, that there's nothing in him to fear.
   Or are you afraid? Exploits of arms were never   750
   what you were known for. Sneaky, rather than brave,
   that's what they call you. You do fear the boy!

ULYSSES: I welcome these insults—which signify
   that you understand now what will happen, accept it,
   and busy the air with words we know are empty.
   The ships are waiting.

ANDROMACHE: Give me at least a moment
   to say farewell to my son, hold him, and weep
   my terrible tears.

ULYSSES: That much, indeed, I can give,
   Had it been within my power, I should have granted
   more, but take your time. With tears and time,   760
   we are able to bear almost impossible burdens.

ANDROMACHE: (*To* ASTYANAX)
   Sweet child, last precious ornament of Troy,
   you were the vessel of our secret hopes,
   and they were right to fear you. When we prayed
   to your father's glorious ghost or your grandsire's,
   it was to you we looked to see their answers,
   but now the last reverberation fades
   to deathly silence, and never shall you wield
   Ilium's royal scepter, nor make the laws,
   nor accept the tribute of conquered nations. Never   770
   shall any of us see the rout of the Greeks, delighting
   to watch them flee your mighty host, nor cheer
   as Pyrrhus's body is dragged in the same dirt
   as your dear father's was dragged in the dust by his.
   I had thought to watch you grow into manhood, playing
   with toys that soon turn real, becoming weapons
   worthy of blood—of game and then of Greeks,
   as the shouts of excited children playing deepen,
   becoming battle cries. . . . O, my sweet son,
   you should have lived longer and better. Death   780
   is often bitter in war, but this is vile.
   No temple altars have you decked; no dance
   have your nimble feet performed; no marriage bed
   have you enjoyed. These grim and broken walls
   have had to watch too much bloodshed already.

ULYSSES: Enough, madam. Your grief goes on forever.

ANDROMACHE: A moment more. A few more tears. . . . My
   hand
   must close his eyes while he still lives and breathes.
   (*To* ASTYANAX)
   Your Troy awaits you. All the heroes are there!

Your father, grandfather Priam, all of them wait   790
to welcome you, a free man, adding your name
to the long list of free and noble Trojans.

ASTYANAX: Mother, help me . . .

ANDROMACHE: Oh, my child, I cannot.
The lion roars, and the calf draws close to its mother's
heaving flank, but the lion feels no pity
and thrusts away the mother to take the tender
defenseless child. So do these animals seize
you from my arms, my breast. My kisses, my tears,
you have.
(*She pulls a few hairs from her head*)
                    And take my hair to your noble father,
and tell him, if ghosts can hear, and feel, and act,   800
to help his poor Andromache. I go
to serve a Greek. Tell him to rouse himself
and fight for me as he used to do. These tears
he will recognize from the day of his death. These
kisses he will know, I think.
(*She kisses him repeatedly, then stops*)
                                   Your cloak,
leave with me as a comfort. Hector's dust
and your warm flesh have touched it, as I will
for comfort, haunting its fabric with my lips.

ULYSSES: (*To his attendants*)
Enough! Take him away. The Argive fleet
has already been waiting long enough.   810

(ULYSSES *and his* SOLDIERS *march off*, SOLDIERS *dragging* AS-
TYANAX *with them.* ANDROMACHE *remains.* CHORUS *enters and sur-
rounds her.*)

CHORUS: Where will they drag us off to? What
   rocky shore, what desolate island,
   distant, and harsh so that flinty souls
   are spawned there?

FIRST CHORISTER: We have heard the names
   of these wild places—Thessaly, Tempe,
   Trachis, Phthia, and Crete. The hordes
   our fathers and husbands fought would speak
   these curious words to indicate "home."
   To us, they mean captivity, exile,
   and the bitter grief of having to mourn   820
   far from the graves of the dead we loved
   and would have preferred to join.

SECOND CHORISTER: We have heard
   their strange stories of places the gods
   have visited, much more often than not
   with evil intent. We are puzzled to hear
   the Greeks recite these stories with pride,
   and their curious boasts of how hard it is
   to approach Calydnae in any wind,
   or how Enispe is always cold
   even in summer, or Calydon   830
   always fears the wild boar's danger.

FIRST CHORISTER: They claim the waters of Titaressos
   arise from the Styx and then flow back
   to return to their dark source, and our hearts
   shudder as if in a cold wind
   to hear such stories.

THIRD CHORISTER: Terrible places,
   but proper perhaps for a woman's grief
   and the hard lesson we've yet to learn
   of acquiescence. They'll lead us away,
   wherever they will and we shall endure   840
   quite indifferent to landscape, threshold,

and face and name of the lord and master
who chose us or to whom we have fallen
by the casting of lots.

SECOND CHORISTER: Still, it is loathsome
to think of going away with Helen
and Menelaus, or Agamemnon,
to live in the citadel of Mycenae,
in Atreus' house and savage Pelops'.

THIRD CHORISTER: My fear is being taken to live
with the crafty Ulysses on Ithaca,   850
or Neritos or tiny Zacynthos,
close-confined as if in a prison,
or worse, penned like an untamed beast.

SECOND CHORISTER: For you, my queen, I cringe to imagine
in what town they will make you a show,
or in what waste field will Hecuba's body
lie, unmourned and even unmarked.

(*Enter* HELEN)

HELEN: (*Aside*) I am the bearer always of terrible news
to the Trojans. Sex and death, mixed up
in the worst way, and it's not at all my fault.   860
I've no choice in the matter, but it seems to happen
over and over. I expect a tepid welcome
at best, and that, only because they fear me,
and rightly: I come to escort Polyxena
to a mock marriage—Pyrrhus is only the stand-in
for the corpse of his great father, with which, too soon,
hers is about to be joined. She doesn't know,
and it's better that way. My job—which isn't pleasant—
is to help her dress as if for her wedding day.
(*To* POLYXENA)
Noble maiden of Troy, I bring you greetings   870
of all the Achaeans, and my own congratulations.

From this disaster, you have been spared, rescued,
to make a match your own father, King Priam,
would approve, I think. Pyrrhus, pride of the Greeks,
has asked for your hand. His illustrious line extends
through Thetis, the great sea goddess, and back beyond
to Olympian Jove. Your dress of somber mourning
you must exchange for the white gown of a bride.
No more a captive, you stand as a woman freed
and the equal now of the greatest, with something old,   880
something new, and a borrowed, blue garter . . .
Your luck has changed. Try to look cheerful, darling. . . .

ANDROMACHE: The one terrible thing we weren't prepared for
is having to "try to look cheerful, darling." Troy's
ruins are still smoking behind us, and she
wants to put on a wedding. But who can refuse?
And what would the penalty be for making objection?
A plague to Greeks and Trojans both, she has only
the dimmest notion of how she is attended
always and everywhere by utter ruin.   890
A marriage! All around, we see the bones
of noble men that carrion birds have picked at
to celebrate one marriage feast or another
of Helen, this monster disguised as a beautiful woman.
A wedding feast! We won't need nuptial torches
with Troy still burning, or any musicians either.
We can dance to groans of the dying and raise our glasses
to a mournful background music of sobs and moans.

HELEN: I don't expect you to like me, but I can't help that.
My conscience is clear. Any sensible person   900
would understand that I've acted as well as I could
in difficult circumstances. You mourn for Hector,
and Hecuba mourns for Priam, and I mourn, too,
for Paris—but secretly, and all alone.
It's hard! And the thing you fear, which is servitude
in a strange country, I have known firsthand
for ten years! Do I get sympathy? Friendship?

Understanding? Nasty remarks are whispered—
always loud enough for me to hear—
wherever I go, among men and women on both   910
sides of the hateful war. Did I deserve this?
None of what happened was my doing! Did Trojans
consult me before they came to Sparta to drag me
away with them? Did Greeks ask my permission
before they launched their ships? A goddess gave me
as prize to Paris, and gods, ever since, have meddled
in these affairs. Blame them! I'm as much a victim
as any of you! My errand here is commanded
by the Great Council. I do what I must, and you
will also do what you must. Andromache, sister,   920
forget for the moment your own sorrows and look
to Polyxena. For her sake, rather than mine—
I can scarcely contain my own tears—try to be brave
and behave yourself with decency, for a change!

ANDROMACHE: You can scarcely contain your tears? Of grief or
        laughter?
    What new trick is in store for us, what new
    treachery do you connive at now? I wonder,
    is it their plan to hurl her off a cliff?
    Or down from the walls? Or drown her out in the bay?
    We're not so easily fooled as once we were,   930
    ten years ago. . . . What evil you bring today,
    I cannot tell, but I know in my belly it's bad.
    Even if what they intend is what you say,
    for Polyxena to wed Achilles' son,
    for Pyrrhus to be the son-in-law of Priam
    is obscene, profane, an outrage! Death would be better.

HELEN: You think I haven't thought of death? You believe
    the path on which I find myself is easy
    or enviable? I take you at your word.
    Do we envy her, supposing she'll be led   940
    like a heifer to Achilles' tomb, and killed
    by the mad hand of Pyrrhus? Do you take comfort

in thinking that she will marry, instead, the father
and her spirit join with his in the underworld?

ANDROMACHE: (*Pointing to* POLYXENA, *who has not flinched or
    even reacted;* HECUBA, *however, faints*)
You see how her noble soul delights to hear
the news of her reprieve. For her, the marriage
would have been a death, and death is a better marriage
than any of us will be forced to undergo.
(*She notices* HECUBA)
Ah, but the poor mother! See how frail
is the thread on which a life can hang! She stirs?   950
Not even Death is a friend to the suffering woman,
but like a coward flees before her grief.

HECUBA: (*Reviving*) I had thought that Paris killed Achilles.
    Dead,
he still harries the Trojans, his very ashes
thirst yet for our blood. I cannot bear it.
Once I had children, many, many children,
clamorous for my kisses. Now there is one,
this single daughter left to me, my comfort
in all the other bereavements I have suffered.
Hers is the only voice that calls for "Mother"   960
and rouses, if for a moment, my numbed spirit,
calling me back to a kind of life. Her death
would free my obstinate soul at last to flee
this broken body and all its earthly torments.

ANDROMACHE: O do not mourn for happy Polyxena.
    Her suffering will be brief, but ours will extend
    for years and miles away from our native land.

HELEN: (*To* ANDROMACHE)
Whether or not you know it, you speak the truth.

ANDROMACHE: What further news do you bring to inflict upon
    me?

HELEN: Lots have been cast, and the women assigned to their
    lords.   970

ANDROMACHE: To whom will I be slave? Out with it! Tell me!

HELEN: The youth of Scyros, Achilles' son—Pyrrhus.

ANDROMACHE: For the first time, I envy the mad Cassandra,
    whom Phoebus exempts.

HELEN: Agamemnon claims her.

(*The women are aghast and, for the moment, silent*)

HECUBA: (*To* POLYXENA)
    Rejoice, daughter! Andromache and Cassandra
    would willingly trade with you.
    (*To* HELEN)
                             But in this raffle,
    has any bold Greek made claim for Hecuba?

HELEN: Ulysses did protest but at last agreed
    to take you as prize—as he said, "for a while."

HECUBA: The shame of it—not servitude but him,   980
    the one who will be my master. "For a while."
    I shall never live to see that barren island.
    What kind of gods can bear to watch old women
    raped and killed by contemptuous, heartless men
    who laugh in their sordid triumphs? This is the world,
    brutal and cruel, that Troy tried to withstand.
    Cruelty wins in the end. Our little clearings
    of civilization may seem real, but mindless
    wilderness always lurks, may take its time,
    but in the end overwhelms all our pretensions   990
    to decency. We revert to beastliness
    and feel, for a moment perhaps . . . regret? Chagrin?
    Their hatred, I feel, too, and pray to the savage

implacable gods to visit pain upon them,
heaving seas, high winds, and raging fires,
wars, betrayals, monsters, and tears, the tears
of envy for Trojans, already dead and safe
from further hurt.
(PYRRHUS *enters*)
                          Ah, Pyrrhus, welcome!
It's not a trick. We are glad you have come to serve us
with a kind of kindness. Here, plunge your sharp sword   1000
into my breast. Old women are no more trouble
to murder than old men!
(*Pointing to* POLYXENA)
                          But you want her,
the little girl. By all means, take her away,
drag her, alive, as your father dragged her brother's
sorry corpse. And may all you Greek brutes
pay for these defilements with your thousand
ships broken, sunk, lost with all hands.

(PYRRHUS *drags* POLYXENA *away.* HELEN *follows.*)

FIRST CHORISTER: The sharing of grief is a solace: the heart's
    hurt is soothed by the recognition
    in other hearts of the same bruise.   1010
    That we are not alone is a comfort
    as voices of dirges and moaning merge
    to become one voice that mourns for the world
    and how it works for everyone,
    rudely and roughly. To be alone,
    picked out somehow for special torment,
    is difficult to endure—but the common
    lot of men and women is grieving.

SECOND CHORISTER: We therefore huddle together to share
    in a biting cold the warmth of our bodies'   1020
    fragile meat. Away with the rich,
    lucky, and happy, whose celebrations
    will quickly enough come to an end

but meanwhile affront us and what we know
of life and the world, which is to say
of suffering and somehow enduring.

THIRD CHORISTER: Whatever the whims of fortune dictate,
    we have to hold on to something solid—
    surely not wealth or power and not
    the ones we loved, whom death can take,   1030
    but the bedrock truth of what we have seen
    and heard and felt—the truth of our grief.

SECOND CHORISTER: Even this bitter sharing of comfort
    will be snatched from us by their rough hands,
    as one by one they put us aboard
    ships bound for their various harbors.
    Never again will two of us meet
    to affirm what we know is in each other's
    hearts, what no one else in the world
    but Trojan women can even imagine.   1040

FIRST CHORISTER: Mount Ida, behind us, will disappear
    into the distance, and in the world
    from then on there will be a hole,
    as large as the mountain, that could have been torn
    from living flesh. To this shore tourists
    will come and look about and gawk,
    poke in the rubble, kick at the scrub,
    and try to imagine that once a city
    stood with its battlements thrusting upward
    into an empty and unremarkable   1050
    patch of sky, and this was Troy.

(*Enter* MESSENGER)

MESSENGER: (*To* HECUBA)
    Ten years of war, and in all that time, no outrage,
    no vileness matches these I must report. . . .
    But which one first? Andromache's or yours?

HECUBA: Whatever terrible news you bring is mine.
　Each feels the weight of her particular woe,
　but I feel all. For me, the whole world dies,
　groan by groan, and always wounding me.

MESSENGER: The boy has perished, thrown from the tower. The
　　girl
　is also dead. Both met their fates most bravely.　　　　　1060

ANDROMACHE: I fear to hear the story but cannot help it:
　we torment ourselves, grasping at these details
　as if there were some cure in them. Tell us!

MESSENGER: You know the tower still standing, Priam's tower,
　　from which he would watch the progress of fighting, direct
　　the troops, and issue orders. On that tower,
　　holding his grandson nestled in his arms,
　　he would point out to the boy the helmet Hector
　　wore, and the two would follow the chase as the hero
　　pursued some terrified Danaan soldier　　　　　　　　　1070
　　who fled for his life, and the lad rejoiced to see it.
　　The wall is gone, but the tower remains, a stronghold
　　in some dreamscape with unruly throngs around it,
　　cheerful as at a fair. They stream from the ships
　　and mill about on the nearby hillside to see,
　　from the peak, between the laurel tree and the beech,
　　that battlement. The two lone trees thrust up
　　as from a brushland; those scrubby plantings between
　　are Greeks, swarming, chatting among themselves,
　　eating and drinking, sitting on Hector's tomb.　　　　　1080
　　　Then, through the crowd, Ulysses makes his way,
　　leading by the hand the boy who follows
　　in confidence to that long familiar spot.
　　They climb the broken stairs. Astyanax
　　stands where he used to stand, at the parapet,
　　looks down at the cheerful crowd. Does he understand?
　　One cannot say. His face is impassive, as once
　　his grandsire's must have been. The crowd is hushed,

solemn, and here and there one can see tears
that fall from brimming eyes. Ulysses recites   1090
the prayers Calchas instructed, summoning gods
to witness what is being done. . . . But the boy,
knowing what then must come, of his own free will,
departs from the script to take command himself
and steps abruptly out, and over, and into
thin air to fall, and plunge in an instant down
through the delicate surface of earth to rejoin Priam
in the gloomy kingdom below. . . .

ANDROMACHE: What fur-clad savage
from the distant desert or furthest Asian steppes
where wild Scythians ride their bareback ponies   1100
could imagine such a barbarous thing? What crude
primitive from Colchis, where they are said
to worship brutal gods in dismaying rites
where babes are fed to hungry cattle, could match
this moment for sheer bloody-mindedness?
My poor child! Who will gather his broken
limbs together to lay them in earth with a decent
burial service?

MESSENGER: There's little left to bury.
He was smashed to bits by the fall. The skull cracked open.
The brains are a pink smear on the rocks below.   1110
He is mere meat.

ANDROMACHE: He is like his father, then.

MESSENGER: (*Taking a breath*)
After the boy had fallen, the throng of Greeks,
still weeping for what had been done in their name,
turned to Achilles' tomb by Rhoetium's waters.
With what thoughts? Who can say? The future threat,
if ever there was a threat, had disappeared.
Would another death propitiate the winds
or offend the gods as it would seem to offend

any sane person watching? They do not speak,
feeling no need. These thoughts are as thick as the dust   1120
that hangs in a granary's air. But there's a drum
and torches, a procession, as at a wedding.
All heads turn to Helen leading the way
as matron of honor, her head bowed and her face
solemn indeed. So may her own young daughter,
Hermione, whom she bore to Menelaus,
be wed one day! There is a certain respect
with which the people look, scarcely believing,
as the bride marches toward the altar, proud
and beautiful—not even Helen's presence   1130
can distract the eyes from lovely Polyxena.
The sun, the moment before it sets, is best,
heartbreakingly splendid, as she is, too,
filling the dimness and looming large in the sky
of consciousness, for we know they will disappear
for all time—her beauty, youth, and courage,
though that will last in our memories the longest.
     Pyrrhus follows. Horror and pity mix
in every heart, as he reaches the steep mound
and faces the brave bride with his naked blade.   1140
She does not turn away, and Pyrrhus is slow
to move, strike, bury his sword to the hilt.
Only then is quickness: of blood spurting,
and the girl falling as if to accuse the earth
and make her reproachful thud on Achilles' grave.
Greeks and Trojans weep together, appalled,
as the blood soaks into the thirsty earth
that drinks the copious gore until it is gone.
Thus was the rite performed.

HECUBA: Now go, you Greeks,
back where you came from. The wind is shifted at last,   1150
and your ships can spread their sails and plough the seas
they lusted for, as you have lusted for blood.
A small boy and a young girl! With their deaths
you bring this disgraceful war to its grisly close.

Where shall I take my grief? What earth will drink
my bitter tears? Where can I go to taint
the air with these last days of a hateful life?
For whom do I mourn—those I have lost, my husband,
children, and grandchild? Or for myself,
the last and loneliest member of Priam's house?   1160
To everyone else, death has been most attentive,
coming before it was called, but me, it shuns,
and I am the one who longs for it most, who wishes
at every moment of daylight, through each long night,
that these rattling breaths could stop at last, that the beating
of this exhausted heart would no longer cause me
throbbings of exquisite pain each moment brings
in which I continue conscious. I stood near Priam,
and not an arrow, not a firebrand
but whizzed by harmlessly, and every miss   1170
now seems a mortal wound.

MESSENGER: I'm afraid it's time.
   The vessels are prepared. They're ready to hoist
   their sails. You must go to the harbor and board the ships.

(*The women file out.* MESSENGER *follows. The curtain falls.*)

THYESTES

THYESTES

CHARACTERS

TANTALUS' GHOST, grandfather of Atreus and Thyestes, he is
    punished in the underworld for having killed his son Pelops,
    whose body he then served to the gods
FURY, who forces Tantalus back to earth to inspire his house to
    further sins
ATREUS, a son of Pelops, he is king of Argos and brother of
    Thyestes
ATTENDANT of Atreus
THYESTES, a son of Pelops, he is the brother of Atreus who has
    been driven into exile
TANTALUS, son of Thyestes
PLISTHENES, son of Thyestes (mute part)
THIRD SON of Thyestes (mute part)
MESSENGER
CHORUS of Mycenaeans
SERVANTS of Atreus (mute parts)

SCENE: *A courtyard of the palace of Mycenae in Argos.*

(TANTALUS' GHOST *is revealed downstage, and also, in half-light and
farther back,* FURY. *Even more dimly lit and farther upstage,*
ATREUS, *the king, is seated, his chin propped in his palm and his
elbow resting on a chair arm. He is meditating, either attending to*
TANTALUS' GHOST *or else inventing him.*)

45

TANTALUS' GHOST: Who calls me from the infernal regions, who
    drags me back, plucks at my tortured spirit,
    to grab at me as I have been grabbing at empty
    air? What worse ordeals have the judges of hell
    devised for Tantalus' Ghost? Hunger in plenty,
    and thirst in the midst of running water are hard,
    as my parched lips can testify. But I've learned,
    barely, to bear these torments. Whatever new
    comes to me now cannot be better! A heart
    of stone would melt at the thought of anything further   10
    heaped on the burden I already carry. The light
    dazzles my dimmed eyes; I tremble with dread
    to return to the world again, where my clan is swarming,
    a multitude, each of whom bids fair
    to make those crimes for which I suffer forever
    trivial, almost innocent compared
    with what they do and dare. Whatever space
    is not yet filled in the land of the damned, whatever
    cell is unassigned by the terrible judges,
    my children and their children shall lay claim to   20
    with the right of terrible wrongs, so long as my house,
    Pelops' damnable house, stains the light
    that assaults my vision.

FURY: That's it, villain. Goad
    your heirs to madness! Let there be competition
    among your issue to exceed one another in guilt.
    Let swords be drawn on this side and that. Let passions
    know neither bounds nor shame. May fury egg
    all of them on to hatred, of parents for children
    and children's children and the other way round. The egg
    will hatch sooner or later monstrous evil,   30
    evil on evil compounded, its reasons confounded
    and altogether surpassed. A kingdom will fall
    and the king will scarcely notice, his glittering eyes
    fixed on the brother he hates, a slave to vengeance.
    Your house will be an asylum for madmen, violent,
    blustering, bragging, and then, in a moment, cringing,

crooning, and desolate—power and wretchedness changing
madly as in a lunatic's wavering fancies.
Chance, stone blind, will lead on a treacherous path
as your heirs are exiled for vile misdeeds and return   40
to worse crimes. But no onlooker will pity
or feel for them anything other than sheer
disgust, while in that arrogant house, in hatred
and fear, brother will mistrust brother, as father
will fear his sons, who will quail at the sight of their father.
Born in disgrace, they will die in an earned vileness.
A wife will strike the blow to dispatch her husband,
and blood will flood the land to bring forth lusts
like vermin, corrupting every virtue. The sky,
clear and pure overhead, will here seem tainted,   50
the stars themselves winking and leering, as spite
and slaughter wheel and settle on Tantalus' house.
Then let them deck the votive pillar with laurel,
hang green boughs on the portals, and light the festal
torches to welcome Tantalus home and do him
reverence. Men will respect this place as a shrine,
the holy of unholies, for here the worst
and bloodiest crimes in mankind's dismal annals
will be outdone. Your grandson Atreus sits
brooding now the cloudy thoughts that will stain   60
the ground with blood. From the delicate pulse that throbs
in his motionless wrist temblors will come to topple
the citadel's walls. That hearth's embers some servant
will fan into blood-red flame, and its cauldron will seethe
unspeakable evils. You say you are hungry? Feast
on the gory banquet we have prepared, and drink
deep of the bloodied wine till your belly is full!

TANTALUS' GHOST: I beg you, let me go back to my pools of
    recoiling
waters, back to that tree that teases and shrinks
just out of reach. Should that seem insufficient,   70
consign me, instead, to Phlegethon's currents of fire,
and there I shall frisk like an otter, sing like a bird,

and let my fellows in suffering know they are blessed
to endure no more than the torments their sins have earned
   them.
Who lies beneath an unstable cairn of boulders
awaiting their crushing blow, let him rejoice!
Who faces the gaping maws of ravening lions
poised to pounce, or shudders to see the Furies
advancing toward him with fiery brands extended,
let them bid welcome to these proportionate trials,   80
glad not to be Tantalus, thrust back
into the land of the living.

FURY: Goad them on:
  in hatred and lust, they finger the hilts of their swords,
  warming their passions, savage, blind, and mad—
  a terrible thing in rulers.

TANTALUS' GHOST: I have learned
  to be torture's victim, not its henchman. I cannot
  bear it that I have become a visitation,
  a pestilence infecting my grandchildren
  and then, through them, the city at large. No,
  I will not do it! To the high gods I cry out   90
  to set some limit to what mankind may suffer.
  I will not hold my piece. I shall defy
  the Fates and Furies, will warn them myself, speak out
  to keep their hands from such an evil thing.
  (*Addressing* ATREUS)
  The holy altars ought not to be so defiled
  by a madman's crime and the innocent blood of children.
  (*To* FURY)
  Do you think your scourges can frighten me? Can serpents'
  writhings do worse than the knottings of my stomach
  in hunger and the burning of my thirst?

THE FURY: Yes, this rage, it's just what we want. Let its fire   100
    light your house! The deep thirst you have felt,
    let them feel too—for one another's blood.
    The walls of the castle tremble at your approach
    as if the stones themselves recoiled in horror.
    Your loathsome spirit presides. As a blessèd presence
    can grace a hill, a grove of trees, or a house,
    you have brought disgrace to all of Argos,
    but most of all to this particular dwelling.
    You have done destiny's bidding. It is enough!
    The earth can no longer endure your presence. Go back   110
    to your accustomed caves in the underworld
    lest the waters here also retreat and the fruits
    of generous trees wither. See how the winds
    harry the clouds along in an ominous sky!
    The trees are nervous, and in your presence their fruit
    withers. The isthmus churns, but the local rivers
    choke on themselves as if their currents gasped.
    The frosts on Cithaeron have fled, as if Phaëthon
    had returned to parch all Argos, and Titan falters,
    unwilling to launch the sun on this odious day.   120

(CHORUS *enters, a mixed group, some male, some female, some of
them wearing togas, others dressed in modern dinner clothes as if at
an opening night at the theater.*)

CHORUS: (*Speaking at first in unison*)
    If any god has ever regarded this place
    with love, or affection, or even attention, if any
    spirit has found some respite here in these gentle
    streams, let him come back here now, for pity's sake,
    to prevent a crime beyond imagination
    from happening here.

FIRST CHORISTER: (*He is one of those in dinner clothes*)
    Unspeakable perhaps,
    but not, alas, beyond imagination.

SECOND CHORISTER: (*He is in a toga*)
    I'm afraid you're right. What we dread, we can surely imagine,
    as that one there imagines and even savors
    its every ghastly detail.
    (*He points to* ATREUS, *upon whom the light now shines more*
      brightly)

FIRST CHORISTER: These old Greek   130
    stories have helped us imagine terrible deeds.

SECOND CHORISTER: Or allow us now to allude to current events
    and speak, albeit in code, of the actions of people
    in power here in Rome. A grandfather's crimes
    taint the lives of grandsons, whose greater crimes
    astonish lesser, less fastidious men.

THIRD CHORISTER: A brother betrays his brother who kills his
    brother.

CHORUS: (*In unison again*)
    There ought to be limits to wickedness. Bonds of affection
    that animals recognize, we, human beings,
    ought to acknowledge. Tantalus' dreadful spirit   140
    infects not only the Argive plain but the whole
    earth, and all of us suffer, for humankind
    knows now what depths have been plumbed and may be again.
    The innocent child Pelops runs to his father,
    in joy to welcome Tantalus home, and his cries
    of delight become abruptly the cries of anguish,
    his and ours as well, that any father can skewer
    his own child.

SECOND CHORISTER: Some in the audience may
    find that their thoughts wander away from the horrors
    before them on stage to others they have not seen   150
    but know about, as one knows of a dead body
    malodorous, rotting somewhere nearby. Who doubts
    that Nero arranged to have his adoptive brother

killed, or that he and mother Agrippina
arranged for Claudius Caesar's murder—his father
at least by adoption? To entertain such thoughts
even in silence is dangerous; to pronounce
aloud what everyone thinks would be sheer madness.

FIRST CHORISTER: It crosses our minds, nevertheless, that Nero's
    childhood tutor and then confidential adviser   160
    was Lucius Annaeus Seneca, this evening's
    playwright.

THIRD CHORISTER: One cannot ignore the coincidences.

CHORUS: Tantalus' penance hardly atones for the bloody
    wounds he inflicted that ooze still in the soul
    of every man. Although we may dream of justice,
    we cannot believe it—except as a children's story
    our grandparents might have told us, who could not bear
    that we should learn too soon the unpleasant truths—
    prime among which is that even one's own grandparents
    cannot be trusted. Minos was judging for us   170
    when he condemned the transgressor to such baroque
    and complicated atonements. We would ourselves
    make such a decree, to let Tantalus scoop
    from the current and bring to his thirsty villain's lips
    nothing! Let him drink from a handful of dust.

(CHORUS *retires to seats at either side of the stage. There, as part of
the audience, they watch while* ATREUS *raises his head and looks out
to the auditorium.*)

ATREUS: O villain, O incompetent, inept,
    and—worst of all for a king—O unavenged!
    Of so many crimes have I been victim,
    enduring a brother's treacheries, my disgrace
    is vile, worse than his guilt, which is limitless.   180
    And I do nothing, stew in useless complaint
    when the whole world should resound with the clash of arms.

There should be scenes of violence and wails of grief
in desolate cityscapes the flames have made
memorably garish. Drawn swords should gleam
where they are yet unsmirched by the gouts of blood
that have not yet recompensed my offended honor.
The countryside should resound with horses' hoofbeats
and cries of the wounded and dying—their proper reward
for having sheltered my wicked brother. Wherever   190
he lay his hateful head, let there be heads
on pikes! These fortress walls bear down, accusing.
Let them collapse upon me, if only their fall
can bury my brother, too, whose moans will soothe
my pains like gentle music. My spirit rouses,
as that of a sick man who drags himself
from his bed to go and vomit. I must dare
something atrocious, spectacular, so bloody,
and altogether beastly that my own brother
will be driven to envy, even as he suffers   200
its dire effects. His proud spirit will break,
as mine will heal to see it. The gory pudding
stands on the banquet table. We must serve
each other and ourselves.

(*Atreus' ATTENDANT enters and makes a formal bow*)

ATTENDANT: And public opinion?
  Do you count that as nothing?

ATREUS: The point of being a king
  is exactly this: that whatever the people cannot
  praise in your actions, they have to endure.

ATTENDANT: When fear
  can compel their praise, it can also make them angry.   210
  Your good repute must be found in their hearts as well
  as upon their obedient tongues.

ATREUS: Any poor fool
  can deserve sincere praise. Only the strong
  can wring it from the reluctant. Let them cheer
  for what they despise!

ATTENDANT: Let the king do right,
  and all his people will cheer him.

ATREUS: But do I care?
  Do you think I want to be king on sufferance? Let them
  suffer whatever they must and, first of all, me.

ATTENDANT: Without honor and virtue, what is a throne?

ATREUS: I sit where I please, and any chair I honor   220
  becomes a throne!

ATTENDANT: But sir, it is still wrong!
  You cannot do such harm to your own brother!

ATREUS: Whatever is wrong to do to a brother, I
  shall do to him, and be right to do it. The black
  stain of his crimes against me leaves not even
  a chink of light for mercy or grace to shine through.
  He debauched my wife and then he stole my kingdom,
  snatching the ram with the golden fleece, that symbol
  of all our power the oracle said would keep us
  secure on the throne. Sacred, alone, it grazed   230
  in a meadow surrounded with high stone walls my brother
  breached. He fouled my bed and chair and smirched
  the honor of this house. I was cast out
  to wander the earth in exile. What kept me alive
  all that time was the dream of doing harm
  to him who had done me harm. There was nothing else
  I could trust, not even my own sons, who could be
  his. I have brooded for years upon revenge,
  and its time has come. I must put on my courage
  and dare what Tantalus dared and Pelops, defying   240

every craven, decent instinct that stays
the clenched fists of most men. But mine will strike
to cause him the foulest hurt it can inflict.
Only say how. In what way shall I wound?

ATTENDANT: Hack with a sword so that his spirit spews?

ATREUS: You leap ahead to the result. Before that,
there is the pain itself, that will make him wish
for death to come as a merciful gift.

ATTENDANT: Disgusting!
Does piety mean nothing to you?

ATREUS: Nothing!
In our house, it has never counted for much.   250
Let the Furies, Erinys and Megaera,
come, brandishing torches further to heat
my frenzy. Unbearable horror is what I want!

ATTENDANT: What mad scheme are you hatching?

ATREUS: Unprece-
                                                     dented
woe! There is no crime in mankind's annals
to satisfy me. This must surpass them all!

ATTENDANT: Not the sword?

ATREUS: It is not enough!

ATTENDANT: Then, fire?

ATREUS: Still, not enough.

ATTENDANT: But what weapon is left?

ATREUS: Thyestes will be the weapon.

ATTENDANT: That would make it
worse.

ATREUS: Worst! I tremble with rage and my heart   260
races, and what I need to soothe my spirit,
to stop the ground from shaking, to keep the sky's
lightning bolts from crashing upon our heads,
and the household gods from turning away in disgust
is that man's exquisite, unendurable pain!

ATTENDANT: What will you do?

ATREUS: Something huge and awful
I cannot yet imagine, but I can feel it
growing in my hands that tingle with it.
My lively fingers quiver. I cannot name it,
but it calls out to something in my soul   270
that answers, "Yes, so be it! Let Atreus do
what his brother has deserved. Let each perform
his part in the dreadful rite." In Thrace, they say,
there was once an unspeakable sacrifice and a feast
of infamy beyond man's imagination.
I speak of Philomel, Procne, and the evil
king they repaid, serving so well. Their rage
is what now fills my soul, as I will fill
Thyestes' belly full. Let the father tear
the flesh from his sons' bodies and let him drink   280
the blood of his blood and gnaw the bone of his bone.
This *amuse gueule* I'll prepare for him, so that he
may carry out with his own gory hands
my dire sentence. Then let him hate himself
with something like my own hot hatred.

ATTENDANT: How
do you propose to entrap him? How will you bring him
willingly into the city where you, whom he fears,
sit on the throne?

ATREUS: I could not manage it
  without his help, but he is a schemer, ambitious,   290
  deceitful, full of guile. In his own snares
  I'll let him entangle himself. He will brave the heavens'
  worst rages, and mine, if he sees some profit,
  and particularly some dishonest profit
  that may accrue.

ATTENDANT: But whom will he trust? On what
  will he rely to take such risks?

ATREUS: His hopes
  will be enough to persuade him. To them, he'll listen
  like a credulous child. I'll give my sons the message
  to carry to their uncle—that the exiled stranger
  may now come home to share in the rule of Argos.   300
  Thyestes, should he spurn my offer, will hear
  his innocent children's pleadings as they repeat
  their cousins' invitation. He'll be moved,
  for their sake if not his own, and his thirst for power
  will aggravate his sense of his own wrongs,
  that he should suffer while I thrive. . . . He will yield.

ATTENDANT: He has learned by now to bear his troubles.

ATREUS: No,
  his sense of having been wronged only increases,
  irritating the galled place.

ATTENDANT: Must you send
  your children to do this deed?

ATREUS: Why not? All children   310
  love to play games. Let them learn to dissemble!

ATTENDANT: What kind of men will they be, having learned such
    lessons?
What if they were to turn one day on you
or Argos?

ATREUS: They would learn sooner or later.
    The throne, itself, would teach them. In any event,
    they were born evil, heirs of an evil house,
    whether they're his or mine.

ATTENDANT: But will you tell them
    the message they bring is a ruse, a part of a trap?

ATREUS: No, for the lessons of silence are hard to learn.
    Only the ills of our lives can instruct us in them.   320

ATTENDANT: But they will have learned deceit from their own
    father,
for you are deceiving them.

ATREUS: For their own good,
    that they may be free from the blame of the heinous crime
    I have in mind. What is the good of spreading
    the guilt to them? A part of my own soul shrinks
    from what I'm about to do. If Agamemnon
    and Menelaus assist me in this deed,
    I shall reclaim them, for they will think themselves mine,
    beyond question: doubt would open the door
    to the burdens of parricide. Sooner than that,   330
    they'll choose to believe they played a part in the murder
    of an evil uncle. I shall not disclose my plan,
    and neither should you, my friend.

ATTENDANT: Oh, I'll keep quiet.
    Fear and loyalty both will be keeping my lips
    sealed. But mostly . . .

ATREUS: Mostly?

ATTENDANT: (*After a slight pause*)   Loyalty.

(ATREUS *laughs. They exit.* CHORUS *rises and walks to center stage. Members seem to confer among themselves for a few moments, nodding and gesticulating, and then they speak.*)

CHORUS: Peace, at last, between the brothers!
   The long years of spite and madness
   come to an end. The skies clear
   in a new dawn of understanding   340
   that riches and power don't make a throne.
   True kingship has nothing to do
   with Tyrian robes or jeweled tiaras.
   A king is that man who knows no fear,
   whose heart is free of the restless longings
   ambition and envy prompt in men.
   The love of the mob is fickle and therefore
   worthless. Treasure is momentary,
   something to count but never to count on.
   In spite of the gaudy wheel of fortune's   350
   turnings the king is never dizzied
   or dazzled. Indifferent to hardships, he holds
   his lands and indeed his life lightly,
   serene as if immortal and glad
   to meet whatever fate may come.

FIRST CHORISTER: The true nobleman earns his title
   from the hard campaigns he has fought alone
   in the small hours, subduing his own
   baser nature. Having conquered
   himself, he has nothing left to fear   360
   from what the capricious world can do.

SECOND CHORISTER: Fear and desire make us villains,
   but he has freed himself from such
   tyrannous masters. He needs no horses,
   armed soldiers, or show of state,

just as he fears neither traitors nor spies.
His steadied soul is a stronger fortress
than Parthian catapult can threaten
with huge rocks. Bold Sarmatian
hordes can never hope to besiege it.   370

FIRST CHORISTER: The only true kingdom is that
a man can bestow on himself, from which
he never can be deposed. The world
may beckon, offering pride of power,
but he knows better. The heights are steep
and the views may be fine, but down at the bottom
are mangled bodies to make us aware
of what the costs can be. I pray
only for clear judgment to see
how, in my humble station, I may   380
enjoy untroubled and sweet repose.

CHORUS: Men's lives have been likened to rivers.
Let mine flow in untroubled currents
that keep to the grassy banks. In the showy
rapids and towering falls of the great,
disasters lurk. Their ride is exciting
but how many come in the end to grief.
Better to paddle in quiet waters
dappled by sunlight that drifts through the leaves
of the overhanging trees and enjoy   390
the talk of our friends and the laughter of children.
Until in the lengthening shadows, we drift
into a doze. Happiness' secret
is easy enough for a man to grasp,
provided only he holds it lightly—
to live simply and then, full of years,
learn to let go. It is not death
we fear but the leaving of what we've loved.
The lesson is simple enough for children
who learn, each day, to go to their beds   400

and endure without any fear the dying
light that signals the end of a day
that wasn't given but only lent.

(CHORUS *is seated.* THYESTES *enters, accompanied by his three
young sons.*)

THYESTES: How good to see the familiar dwelling places,
   handsome as I remember them. An exile
dreams of this moment, yearns as a blind man would
for the vision of what he holds most dear. But dreams
are not to be trusted. I reach out with my hand to touch
the Cyclopean walls and feel their huge smoothed stones.
One sense confirms the other's report as true,   410
and still I find it hard to believe. I'm home,
can turn to see the racecourse, empty now
and silent, but I can remember the cheering crowds.
Those were my great days, driving my father's
chariot in those races, and winning the palm.
Will they cheer now to see me again? Will they come
to crowd around me? Will Atreus, my brother,
welcome me? Or should I be content
with this one moment, turn away, and hide
in the dark woods, where outlaws live and beasts?   420

YOUNG TANTALUS: (*Aside*) I am afraid. My father's behaving
   strangely.
His step is uncertain, as if he were dazed or ill.

THYESTES: I don't believe my brother's promise. I don't
   trust him. I should never have come. The hardships
I have already learned to bear may prove to be
trivial as compared with what he intends.
It's not too late. I can still turn around, turn back,
having seen the city, and save myself and my sons.

TANTALUS: Why do you hesitate, father? What can be wrong?
  Is this not what you've prayed for all these years?   430
  Now that the blessing falls from heaven, why not
  hold out your hands to receive it? Instead, you defend,
  as if from a blow. What do you fear? Your brother?

THYESTES: I am, indeed, afraid but cannot say
  what it is I fear. I should like to believe, but cannot.
  Something feels wrong. I'm like a laden ship
  making for port, urged on with oars and sails,
  and yet there's a strong tide running, so that I slip
  backward, moment by moment. I feel that tug.

TANTALUS: It's nothing that you can name? Why, then, it's
    nothing.   440
  Think of the prize that waits within these gates.
  Father, you can be king!

THYESTES: Long live the king!

TANTALUS: Think of the wealth and power!

THYESTES: They're nothing to
                                                        me.

TANTALUS: And your sons will succeed you!

THYESTES: A throne seats
                                                    only one.

TANTALUS: Who would choose to be wretched rather than happy?

THYESTES: What has a throne to do with being happy?
  Men suppose that power delights in itself
  and that hardship is something to fear, but I have been
  up there on that giddy height, and the fear
  of falling is what I remember. Down at the bottom   450
  the footing is more secure. To lie on the ground

is safest, and not to have to eat one's bread
in fear of thieves, who prefer to invade mansions.
In golden goblets, there's often poisoned wine,
and you look to your taster, and he looks to your friends,
and on his face is the fear you try not to show.
Believe me. I have been there, and I know.
What we believe to be misfortune carries
certain compensations. No man fears me,
or covets what I have or envies me.   460
My own conscience is clear, for I have not
plundered the earth for more than my fair share
of what it offers mankind. I don't tax
brutish Getae off at the end of the map.
Savages aren't roaming the woods for rare
incense for my lamps or exotic plants
to grow in hothouse tubs to impress my guests.
I never sleep all day or carouse all night,
and I walk the streets without armed men's protection.
Want, as I've learned, is a boundless and peaceable
   kingdom.   470

TANTALUS: But would you refuse a throne a god bestows?
   Your own brother invites you to share the kingdom!

THYESTES: Invites? That scares me. Some gift horses bite.

TANTALUS: The affection that brothers feel is like a stream
   that runs underground for a time but then must surface.

THYESTES: My brother loves me? It's not what I'd expected
   any more than I'd thought to see fire and water
   come to terms, or life and death commingle,
   or the fickle winds steady themselves to faith
   and wed the restless sea. Sicilian tides   480
   will sooner lie there motionless and bring forth
   fields of ripening grain in the midnight's dazzle!

TANTALUS: But what betrayal is it you fear?

THYESTES: Betrayal
   itself. His hatred is boundless as his power.

TANTALUS: What can he do to you?

THYESTES: To me? Nothing.
   But I fear what he can do to you, my sons.

TANTALUS: You're already on your guard.

THYESTES: What good does
                                               that do,
   once you have fallen into the pit? On guard?
   Impaled on spikes, more like. But lead the way.
   I'll follow, for your sake, but I won't lead.   490

(ATREUS *enters, sees* THYESTES *and his three* SONS, *and gloats at
having them in his power*)

ATREUS: My victim! Trapped in the nets I've set! The whole
   brood, father and sons together. Hatred
   is bitter but at moments like this can bloom
   with a wonderful sweetness. Hunger pales, and love
   is a wan shadow. My spirit's alive, my heart
   sings. My nerves are on fire, but all in pleasure.
   When the boarhound's on the leash and his muzzle is down,
   he tracks the boar almost in silence, and snuffles
   across the fields, but then, when the quarry is near,
   bells, bays, breaks free, bounds ahead.   500
   He's a trained animal, mind you, but he goes,
   drags his laggardly master along behind him,
   and he's eager for the kill. It's rage, blood lust
   in the sight of blood, and it's just unbearably fine!
   How lovely to gaze at that unlovely face I have longed
   to see before me! How can I hide my feelings?
   And yet, I must, to draw out the pleasure, to keep
   the game going longer.
   (*To* THYESTES)

Hail, good brother!
I rejoice to see you again. Let us embrace
as I have longed to do, all anger gone   510
and only the ties of love to hold us together.

THYESTES: Your goodness shames me, brother. I could contrive
excuses for my wicked deeds, but your
generous welcome undoes me. I've done wrong
and am heartily sorry. In the gleam of your love my sins
seem all the blacker. I have offended virtue
itself, and my tears must plead my case, for no
words will do. My extended hands beseech
that never before reached out like a beggar's to plead.
I clasp your knees, in the hope that you'll put by   520
your righteous anger, and pledge as tokens of faith
my guiltless boys.

ATREUS: Arise, brother. Embrace
not just my knees, but me! And your sons, as well!
Let us hug one another. Put off those vestments
of squalid exile. I hate to see them. Royal
trappings you all shall wear, as fine as my own,
for we shall share together in all things.
I reserve for myself only the glory of giving—
or better, say, of restoring to my dear brother
what is his by right. The wielding of kingly power   530
happens through chance; the bestowing of it, through love.

THYESTES: May the gods repay you. The crown you are kind to
     offer,
but I refuse it. My hand recoils from the scepter.
Let it be mine to blend in as one of the crowd.

ATREUS: The throne's big enough for two.

THYESTES: You may have it all.
My share is yours.

ATREUS: You spurn the gifts of fortune?

THYESTES: I've learned never to trust them.

ATREUS: But will you
                                                      deny me
    the honor of giving? Of sharing?

THYESTES: That's yours already,
    but mine will be in refusing what you have offered.
    There's honor enough for two of us to share.   550

ATREUS: But I lose mine if you don't accept your part.

THYESTES: Very well, I accept the title of kingship—but you
    shall keep the power, and I shall be your subject.

ATREUS: (*Putting the crown upon* THYESTES' *head*)
    Wear, then, this crown I set upon your dear head,
    and I shall perform the sacrifice in your honor.

(*They exit.* CHORUS *rises and confers among themselves.*)

CHORUS: Who can believe such things? The wonder
    of love exceeds our fondest hopes.
    The brothers are reconciled, their anger
    melted like metal in fire. Strangers
    may keep their hatred going, but brothers   550
    are bound to each other forever. It does us
    good to see that it can happen,
    restoring our faith in human kindness.

FIRST CHORISTER: Hatred can come to eclipse the steady
    light of affection's lamp, and in darkness
    men will grope, flail out, afraid
    to show their fear. The world turns hostile,
    and enemies everywhere menace with fleets
    of warships, parading cavalry squadrons,

in battle's terrible panoply.   560
The thirst for blood is a dreadful thirst,
but Love can stay the brandished weapon,
disarm the combatants, take their hands
and join them once more in peace and friendship.

SECOND CHORISTER: See what the god has contrived for us here!
Throughout Mycenae, mothers were frightened
and clasped their innocent babes to their bosoms
as wives feared for their husbands in arms
and awaiting orders. The sword in the corner
that had rusted in peace was glinting bright   570
in the menace of imminent action. The walls
we'd long neglected, we reinforced
and we strengthened the gates with bars of iron.
Worse than war is the fear of war,
but now that cloud is gone from the sky
and a civil peace is restored to the city.

CHORUS: It happens this way, when the raging sea
and whipping wind batter the boats.
The sailors who make for a safe harbor
can hardly imagine that lee shore   580
they struggle to reach beyond the walls
of water that crash down on the decks.
But then, somehow delivered and moored,
they make fast and can barely remember
the salty taste of terror that burned
all that time at the backs of their throats.

FIRST CHORISTER: What emotion endures? Pain
fades, thank heaven, but also pleasure.
Time turns fortunes topsy-turvy,
and he whose head is crowned with laurel,   590
he whose hand is clasped on a scepter,
he will bend his knee and grovel
down in the dust before the man
he'd thought of before as beneath his notice.

SECOND CHORISTER: Let us therefore try to maintain
 our balance, remembering modesty's lesson.
 Success and prosperity come unbidden
 and undeserved, as their opposites also
 happen at random. No one should preen
 in self-congratulation, and no one   600
 ought to despair. Whom the rising sun
 shines on in triumph, the setting sun
 may wash in the long shadows of woe.

CHORUS: Let us all learn these difficult lessons,
 keeping in mind that any power
 must yield in turn to a greater power.
 No man ought to enjoy the moment
 without giving thanks to the gods, who in turn
 acknowledge the Fates' powers. No man
 ought to give in to despair either   610
 for we remember we live like leaves
 on the whim of the fickle winds that any
 moment can bear us up or dash us
 down from whatever height we have clung to
 having persuaded ourselves it is home,
 where we belong and what we have earned.
 Clotho braids the skeins of our lives
 weaving weal and woe together.
 No man, therefore, ought to rely
 on tomorrow or even this afternoon   620
 as the swift wheel of fortune continues
 its dizzying whirl.

MESSENGER: (*Enters in a great hurry*)
                     Good sirs, I beg your pardons.
 I come to tell a fearful thing. A shame!
 Even to Pelops and Tantalus' house, a scandal!
 I can hardly bring myself to impose upon you
 with the dreadful words!

FIRST CHORISTER: (*Patiently*) Sir, tell us your news!

MESSENGER: What kind of world is it, what kind of place
   are we living in, where such vile things can happen?
   Far beyond the pale of civilization,
   out in the Scythian wastes, such monstrous crimes   630
   might, I suppose take place. But this is Greece!

FIRST CHORISTER: (*Less patiently*)
   Whatever this evil is, we pray you, tell us!

MESSENGER: I will, I promise. Once I've composed myself,
   and have mastered my terror, I will. But still, I can see it,
   a ghastly image seared on my eyes. I close them,
   but still that image persists. I would rather flee
   to the other end of the world than impose upon you
   the scar I bear.

FIRST CHORISTER: You impose on us, sir, with doubt!
   Tell us what makes you shudder. Say who did
   this dreadful deed you can barely report. Tell us!   640

MESSENGER: At the topmost peak of the citadel, the palace
   of Pelops looks to the south. You know where I mean,
   where the wall of the mountain becomes the palace wall
   that looks down on the town in what seems like menace,
   daring the insolent townsmen below to return
   its menacing stare. Inside is the great hall there
   splendid with columns painted in all those colors.
   Beyond that hall, the palace extends to the north
   and follows around the hill, but hidden within
   those courtyards, pavilions, and colonnades, at the heart   650
   and innermost retreat, is the ancient grove
   where the old trees are safe from the pruner's knife,
   a bower of yew and gloomy ilex and oak
   towering high overhead. Into that quiet
   shaded place, the sons of Tantalus come
   in moments of grief or doubt, for calm and solace,
   and here, too, they have hung their votive gifts:
   war trumpets, fragments of chariots, trophies

of battle. The place, we may say, is a private shrine,
and in its silence one may imagine the cries   660
of warfare as well as other and worse outrages—
crimes of the tribe, for example. The coronet
in the Phrygian style of Pelops is hanging there,
along with his richly embroidered robe. In the shade,
a spring arises, bubbling water as dark
as if from the Styx itself, on which the gods
are said to take their oaths. There are also stories
of how, at night, in the darkness, there at the pool
the spring has made, you can hear moans of the dead
welling up from the source of those deep waters.   670
Ghosts are said to howl, and terrible creatures
that never lived make frightening visitation,
chilling the marrows of rationalists and skeptics.
Flashes of eerie light float through the air,
and the branches of trees flicker and glow, inflamed
but there's no fire. Howls that could be from dogs
resound in dissonant clamor, but no dog's there.
The rooms of the palace that overlook that grove,
nobody uses. At night the place is a horror,
but even at dawn the taint persists, continues   680
as if night clung to the trees that were sanctuary,
even at high noon, to the sinister spirits.
Here, the oracle speaks, announcing the Fates
in a pained moan. And here, Atreus came,
dragging his brother's sons to the decked altars. . . .
But who could describe, who could believe what happened?
He binds their hands behind their backs. They let him.
What do they know? He drapes the purple braiding
upon their foreheads. They still have no idea
that anything's odd. There's incense, wine, a knife,   690
and the salted meal to sprinkle over the victims.
It's all correct, an observance of ritual, only
where are the victims? The ox? The unblemished lamb?

FIRST CHORISTER: Who takes the knife in hand?

MESSENGER: He does,
                                                  himself.

    He serves as the priest, officiating, himself
    at the nightmarish rite, that vile and bloody observance.
    He chants the dirge as the grove begins to tremble,
    its balefulness now surpassed by the ceremony
    that now befouls it further, forever. The earth
    shudders as if in revulsion from what happens,   700
    and the skies recoil, meteors shooting their murk
    in the sinister quarter. He sets them upon the altar
    and pours the wine upon the burning fire,
    but the wine as it spills is turning to clotted blood.
    The crown on the king's head slips, falls down,
    and he puts it back, but it slips again and again.
    The ivory statues weep in dreadful portent,
    but Atreus is not moved. He seems to be pleased,
    defying the menacing gods with prayers like curses.
    Only his eyes move as he stands at the altar   710
    looking at this one and that, like a Ganges tigress
    that cannot decide which of a herd of bullocks
    to pounce on first with bared and terrible fangs.
    He hesitates, or perhaps just savors the moment,
    delightfully pregnant, knowing it will bring forth
    savage revenge.

SECOND CHORISTER: And which one does he strike?

MESSENGER: The pride of place goes to the eldest, the nephew
    who bears the grandfather's name—it's Tantalus first.

FIRST CHORISTER: How did he bear this terrible death?

MESSENGER: How?
    He did not plead. He knew all prayer was vain.   720
    The king thrust in with the sword, making a wound
    so deep the hand on the sword hilt touched the skin
    of the young boy's neck. He pulled the blade back out,
    and the corpse still stood for a moment, upright, balanced,

and wavering crazily, as if to choose which way
it wanted to fall. Then it collapsed on the uncle.
He let it fall to the ground and dragged Plisthenes
to the same altar and cut the head off clean.
It rolled away, its mouth agape in a scream
that made not even the shadow of any sound.   730

FIRST CHORISTER: And after this double murder, did he not spare
    the third, the youngest child? Could he show no mercy?

MESSENGER: They say a lion that falls on a herd will kill
    even after its hunger is sated. The blood
    acts like a drug to put the beast in a frenzy
    to kill, crazy with gore and eager for more
    and more. And I can believe it, having seen
    how Atreus, now pure savagery, turned on the third
    and, waving the bloodied sword overhead, struck,
    driving clear through the body. The sword point entered   740
    beneath the lad's sternum, and came out near the spine.
    He fell on the already bloodied altar, and new
    blood flowed from both wounds.

FIRST CHORISTER: Beyond belief!

MESSENGER: You're horrified? If the crime had ended there,
    that would have been—in relative terms—a blessing.

FIRST CHORISTER: In relative terms? What are you saying? What
    worse
    can we even imagine?

MESSENGER: But Atreus had imagined,
    and thus far it was only the preparation.

FIRST CHORISTER: What else could he do? Throw their mangled
    corpses
    to the scavenging beasts? Deny them the rites of the
    dead?   750

MESSENGER: O, would that he had done so! If only dogs
   had gnawed their bones! What happened is so much worse
   that what you consider dreadful appears to me
   the dream of pity itself. Better that crows
   should have pecked their flesh. The declension of horror is such
   that some of the smaller outrages become
   pleasant to contemplate. Their bodies thrown
   in a ditch by the side of the road where their father could see
      them . . .
   that would have been no more than a lapse of decorum
   compared to this. Atreus sliced them open,   760
   tore out their quivering vitals, the little hearts
   twitching with life's last spark. Then, like a butcher,
   he hacked the limbs from the trunks, cracked their bones,
   and stripped off the flesh he fixed on cooking spits
   and set on the fire to turn and drip. Their organs
   he tossed into kettles to stew over fires that gagged
   at what they were made to do. The livers sizzled,
   and the logs beneath them crackled in an outraged
   antiphon beyond all imagination.
   The smoke that rose was black and pitchy and stung   770
   the eyes as if to remind them what weeping was.
   The sun itself shrank from what it beheld
   and fled the sky, but too late not to witness
   the noxious feast Atreus brought to the table.
   The father carves his sons' bodies and chews
   flesh of his own flesh. He wipes his lips
   with a napkin and takes a sip of wine to wash down
   meat that has stuck in his throat. The single mercy
   for poor Thyestes, at this point, is in his total
   ignorance—and that can't possibly last.   780
   In despair, one tries to imagine time turning back
   to run the other way. The stunned sun shudders
   and flees eastward, undoing what has been done.
   But nothing can blot out these ghastly events.
   The blow has fallen, and what awaits is the pain
   of realization of how the world is sick,
   mad and sick, that such vile things can happen.

There's nothing to do now but wait for the groans.
(*During this speech, the light has been fading almost to
   darkness*)

CHORUS: What kind of world do we live in? How
   does a man bear the brutal blows   790
   a life entails? These evils await us
   like adders, sunning themselves on rocks.
   The sun should flee from the sky, and sky
   shrink from the foul earth beneath it
   before permitting such profanation
   to poison the landscape. Close your eyes,
   but the terrible images still persist
   as if the gates of Hades had opened
   and rotting bodies strolled in the streets,
   their cerements streaming foulness behind them.   800

FIRST CHORISTER: The Giants return to wage their war,
   Tityos wrathful and Typhoeus crazed
   and strong enough to throw off those mountains
   that have held his huge body captive.

SECOND CHORISTER: One need not look so far to find
   parallel cases. At home, in Rome,
   someone has his own half-brother
   poisoned at dinner. Everyone sees
   but says nothing and does nothing.
   Then he murders his own mother,   810
   and nothing happens, nothing at all.
   The sun continues to rise in the east
   and travel its usual course across
   a clear baby-blue heaven, but how?
   Is there no justice? Are there no gods
   to keep such foulness away from the world?

FIRST CHORISTER: A man's soul, sickened to death
   from what he has seen, cries out to whatever
   power he still believes in, protesting
   that nature continues its usual course.   820
   The sun and the moon are indifferent. His own
   body's organs persist in the stupid
   business of living, while all he wants
   is that everything stop, the day, the seasons,
   and his own heartbeat and bitter breath.

SECOND CHORISTER: If life must go on, let it at least
   bear witness to horror. The world should provide
   cataclysms, earthquakes, ruin.
   The caricatures of nighttime horrors
   should walk about in broad daylight.   830
   Those dreary creatures whose unconcern
   affronts the intelligence . . . let them suffer,
   let them share in the general outrage
   and pay in pain for the sin of indifference.
   The walls of houses crack, and the people
   run in the streets, crying in panic . . .
   as well they should. As they ought to have done
   from the very first moment when madness
   seized the world.

FIRST CHORISTER: We know how it is.
   Everything turns around, and evil   840
   becomes the standard. Pain is real
   and everything else is merely a moment
   of respite, irrelevant. Scars are the only
   parts of the body to trust. The rest
   of the smooth and innocent flesh is merely
   waiting to feel the fire, the steel,
   and send the news of pain to the brain,
   which all along was waiting to hear it.

CHORUS: Let us correct the calendar. Feasts
    will be no more, but only fast days 850
    marking the marvels of what we have borne,
    what we have not given into yet,
    although there were moments when each of us prayed
    for release at last from the trials and torments.
    The coming of spring, the heat of summer,
    the time of harvest in autumn, the cold
    winter weather in one or another
    occasions some recollection of grief
    the look of the day brings back. He holds
    his hand to his jaw as if he had toothache, 860
    or buries his head in his arms in pain.

FIRST CHORISTER: Perhaps the gods are only preparing
    that dreadful cleansing they have it in mind
    to visit upon us. One learns to long
    for such a conclusion, when every blade
    of grass is an outrage, a green affront.
    One wants the satisfaction of seeing
    justice done. However oppressive
    the penalties are, the world deserves
    more and worse. The life we hate 870
    wants some extravagant extirpation.

CHORUS: Some crimes can be so heinous
    they spread their taint beyond the one
    who struck the blow. The blemish extends
    out of the house and along the decorous
    streets to the fields beyond the gates
    of the town walls. Total strangers
    are guilty of having lived and survived,
    contemporaries of absolute evil.
    Mixed in with our grief is guilt 880
    of the eyes for having seen, of the ears
    for having heard such abomination,
    for what kind of person, receiving such news,
    would not have much preferred to die?

(ATREUS *enters, exulting. He is accompanied by two* SERVANTS.)

ATREUS: I know now how the gods must feel. Their power
  sings along my nerves. I thrill to their giddy
  altitude, as if I peered down from heaven
  to watch as the tiny figures of men scurry
  on what they take to be paths of important purpose.
  I have accomplished all that I prayed to the gods   890
  to let me achieve. What I had longed for and dreamt,
  I saw in the waking world, the father feasting
  on the flesh of his sons. The gods granted my plea
  and then, as if astonished by what they had done,
  fled. No god remains, but only myself,
  my pure will imposing itself on the world
  in all the detail they wanted not to witness.
  It doesn't matter, so long as Thyestes sees,
  and, pleased as I am, my last delight remains
  that perfect consummation of my scheme—   900
  I wait now for the sun of his understanding
  to rise at last in a crimson drawn from the blood
  of his three sons.
  (*To* SERVANTS)
                          Throw open the temple doors
  and let my remarkable banqueting hall be shown.
  (*Again, to himself*)
  I still have the heads to display, to prove the truth
  of words he won't believe from my mouth. Theirs,
  mute now, will incontrovertibly speak.
  And then will his well-fed cheeks turn ashen, pale
  as the blood flees. But I have prepared him drink,
  to restore his strength.
  (*The doors are opened, and* THYESTES *is revealed at table*)
                          It is lovely to be a man,   910
  even better to be a king, but a god,
  immortal, invincible, limitless in the power
  to turn thought to event, that's best of all.
  To see him wretched is gratifying, but still
  it is even better to watch as the wretchedness happens,

the beautiful change as, when an animal, quick
and alive, becomes, amazingly, mute meat.
His dinner done, he toys now with his wine,
blood-red, flavored with real blood, and he drinks!

THYESTES: (*He sits at the banquet table, surrounded by empty*
    plates, and holding a goblet)
To be home at last, safe and secure, 920
all my wanderings past, my woes
almost forgotten . . . I've come to rest,
free of ambition that drove me once
and quite content to enjoy the plain.
The kingdom's riches that tempted me then
seem to have shrunk. Those golden baubles
are nothing but toys. The real riches
are those of the soul, the talent to take
the small satisfactions that come to hand—
or can if it is not clenched to a fist, 930
or clutching a sword's hilt or a scepter.
Still, I am apprehensive, the worries
that hounded me then are faithful still,
and I cannot believe in the peace of the present
moment, the respite. Chance has turned me
skittish and shy like an ill-used dog.
Even here in the palace's safety,
I'm apprehensive. I wait for a blow
to shatter the calm and its pretty illusions.
Do the flowers that wreathe my brow mock me? 940
Too used to bitter tears, I bridle
at what's too strange to be understood.
Will these rich robes I put on be rent
in lamentation? I do not trust them!
I've no reason to fret, no cause
to suspect that the Fates are waiting to show me
my old face in the mirror, contorted
by weeping and ranting, barely human.
Surely the Furies must show me mercy
after such long and faithful attendance. 950

But it doesn't work that way, the talent
one learns from a craft is what one becomes,
and what I have learned as a faithful apprentice
is how to grieve. Like a wary sailor,
I look to a fair sky and a calm
sea and see the portents of storms
coming from nowhere, walls of water
breaking over the puny ships.
I already hear the cries of the drowning
and taste the brine they swallow, salty   960
and bitter as tears. I trust my brother.
Why then does my hand tremble
holding the cup of wine? Why should I
fear that disaster is crouched in the corner
waiting to pounce and fasten its fangs
into my heart? I cannot help it.
Knowing better, I ought to distinguish
between what's real and what I imagine
and learn at last how to be happy.

ATREUS: (*Advancing toward* THYESTES)
    Good brother! Let us keep this day for feasting   970
    for all time and rejoice in the bond of peace
    between us now that secures the throne we share.

THYESTES: I have eaten and drunk my fill of food and wine.
    All that remains to perfect my content and delight
    is that my sons may join in the celebration.

ATREUS: I assure you, they're here. Your sons are with you
        always,
    safe in your bosom. They cannot be taken from you.
    I promise that you and they shall never be parted.
    Those boys will sustain you, nourish and fill you
    with a father's pride. They'll satisfy you, I swear!   980
    I am just now come from the children's table. They share
    in the festive meal. I'll summon them here for you.
    Take, meanwhile, this ancient cup, refilled.

THYESTES: I accept with pleasure your generous gifts. Let wine
    be poured to the household gods and then be drunk. . . .
    But what's the matter? My hand isn't right. The cup
    is heavy, hard to lift. I can scarcely hold it
    or carry the wine to my lips. And the wine's peculiar. . . .
    It doesn't want to be drunk but sloshes and spills
    as if it were something alive. And the candles gutter.   990
    What has come over me? I'm not well. There's something
    terribly wrong. The light is fading, and shadows
    menace. I'm frightened. Whatever it is, I pray
    it may spare my brother. My sons, I hope, are safe.
    The gods are angry with me—I've sins to atone for—
    but my sons are innocent children. Let them be
    brought! I want my children. Please!

ATREUS: I'll bring them,
    and never shall you be parted again, I swear.

(ATREUS *exits*)

THYESTES: I tremble! I'm feeling sick. My heart is beating
    fast, in terror. Are they all right? My children!   1000
    If they are well, I do not fear for myself.
    Where are they?
    (ATREUS *returns with a large salver*)
                You said you'd bring them. Are they safe?

ATREUS: Open your arms to receive them. Here they are.
    (ATREUS *removes the cover*)
    You recognize your sons' adoring faces?

THYESTES: I recognize my brother! Oh, gods!
    How can the earth endure so vile a crime!
    Crack, and let him fall into hell. Chaos
    must snatch him away, the king and kingdom with him.
    The whole damned palace, let it be razed,
    and all of Mycenae. You and I should be dead,   1010
    should have died long ago. This accurséd house

ought to have been exterminated like vermin,
or thrown into some abyss, some bottomless pit
where souls guilty of crimes less heinous than ours
could tread on our heads with their filthy feet. Gods!
But there are no gods! The earth lies there, like a
lump of stupid rock. And the gods have all gone away,
leaving us here abandoned, like little children
suddenly orphaned. We call out, and our voices
echo in emptiness and mock our grief.   1020

ATREUS: But be of good cheer! I have brought the children you
    loved.
You see how your brother obliges. Take them. Kiss!
Nibble their little lips. Embrace all three!

THYESTES: Is this what you swore? Is this your honor? Your trust?
Is this how you put our hate behind us? My brother!
I ask you, nevertheless, a last favor,
which you may grant, hating me nonetheless.
Let me bury their bodies. Give me back
the rest of their corpses that I may see them burned
and perform their rites. You cannot refuse me that.   1030

ATREUS: Whatever remains of them, brother, you have. What
    does not,
you also have.

THYESTES: What is this riddle? Where are they?
Are they prey for the wild birds now? Food for the beasts?

ATREUS: One might say. They were, just now, your dinner.

THYESTES: (*Moans*) It was this that shamed the gods. From this,
    they fled.
And the light fled and the candles guttered. What words
are there? What gods to hear them? I see the heads,
the remains' leavings. Their flesh seethes in my own.
I gag on my crime. Brother give me your sword

that I may cut my belly open and free them.   1040
But a sharp sword from you would be a mercy.
Contrive some other death, then. Crush me with stones.
Do what you will, but release me from this torment.
When I descend to meet the shades, they will shudder
in fear and disgust at what goes on up here
in what they thought was the world of the light. Such crimes
the beasts don't know, nor the savages out in Asia
roaming the rocky steppes. What have I done?
Whatever there was between us, this is wrong,
disproportionate, crazy! Even a crime   1050
ought to have some logic to it.

ATREUS: A crime
ought to have limits beforehand. I agree with you there.
But this is repayment of crime, is vengeance, is different,
and even this isn't enough. I'd have rather
poured the hot blood fresh from their wounds
down your retching throat that you could have drunk
the gore of your still-living sons. I hurried.
It was all too quick, too easy. I drove my sword
into their bodies there at the altar. They died
at once—and never knew what happened after.   1060
They could not see me tear their bodies apart,
didn't watch as I stuck their livers on spits
and roasted them over the fire, could not hear
the sputtering sounds of cooking. And neither did you!
I should have preferred that you watch me prepare your
    banquet,
slicing the meat and arranging it there on the platter.
I should have delighted to see you chew and swallow,
knowing what food you were eating.

THYESTES: O great gods!
How can you not hear this? How can you stand it?
I pray you all, attend. Gods of the earth,   1070
gods of the sky, gods of the sea, see
what has been done here, and not at all for my sake—

for I am beyond all help or comfort—but yours,
for the sake of your own honors, the sake of the world
you rule, send down to us your drastic, cleansing
anger. With fire, burn away this filth!
Set the winds to work to scour this blackness
white again. The sky should blaze with lightning
and the torrents pour to purge and purify
this blot on creation. Let the thunder clap   1080
and show again your fury that undid Giants
and tamed the earth. And do it now! I beg.
Or, better, I defy you. I dare you! Do
to him or me the worst you can do. With flame
of your lightning bolts, strike this breast to burn
in a proper rite the bodies of my three children.
Blaze and cleanse, I say, or admit forever
there's nothing there. Nothing but black space,
in which case we must worship night and cold,
and learn to love death and adore corruption,   1090
for either this is real and all the rest
has been a delusion, a poet's pretty conceit,
a children's story, or else the world we live in
is yours, the real world, and this an offense
unparalleled on earth.

ATREUS: Very nicely said.
   It's sweet music, better than any praise
   I could imagine. My labors are not in vain,
   as they might have been without these complaints of yours
   I delight to hear.

THYESTES: What was my children's sin?

ATREUS: That they were yours. And now are my own sons
         mine,   1100
   restored to me—if you bedded my wife or not.
   Your sons were surely yours, and restored to you.

THYESTES: I call on the gods who protect the innocent.

ATREUS: Gods?
Why not call on the marriage gods?

THYESTES: You punish
a crime with a worse crime.

ATREUS: You're jealous, I think,
and sorry you couldn't have done to me what I
have done to you. But you couldn't. Cook my children
to feed them to me? But what if they were yours?
That was what stayed your villain's hand.

THYESTES: To the gods
I commend you for their eternal curse.

ATREUS: To your sons'   1110
shades I offer you up—as I just offered
them to you. I wish a long life to you all!

(They glare at each other for a moment. Then, blackout.)

PHAEDRA

PHAEDRA

CHARACTERS

HIPPOLYTUS, son of Theseus and Hippolyta
PHAEDRA, wife of Theseus and stepmother of Hippolytus
NURSE of Phaedra
THESEUS, king of Athens
MESSENGER
HUNTSMEN, companions of Hippolytus, and SERVANTS of Theseus
    (mute parts)
CHORUS of Athenians

SCENE: *A courtyard of the palace at Athens.*

(HIPPOLYTUS, *an extremely handsome, scantily clad young man, enters with a company of armed* HUNTSMEN, *one or two of whom have hounds on the leash. He proceeds to give the men their instructions. In the background,* PHAEDRA *stands and watches him, while her old* NURSE *watches her.*)

HIPPOLYTUS: Into the heart of the woods and up
   the sharp slopes to the crests of the hills
   we'll beat the bushes for game. The clever
   beasts take shelter among the crags,
   are poised on the steep inclines, or hide
   in deep gullies, but we will find them.
   You lads of Athens, off to the hunt!
   Others may take the easier paths,

87

stroll through meadows, keeping an eye
peeled for whatever they might surprise,   10
but we'll try harder and do better.
Let those dabblers go for their walks
along Ilissus' banks, where the river
reaches the sea—they'll all come back
with empty pouches. We'll go further
and bring back more. Near Marathon,
where the pass opens into the plain,
there, in the glades, will be good hunting,
beasts abundant, stags and does
and suckling fawns grazing together.   20
There's more pleasure but less profit
to hunt together, so let us spread out,
go our separate ways and cover
more ground. Let one of us try
to Acharnae, another Hymettus' cliff,
and yet a third to little Aphidnae.
A few should venture even as far
as Sunion, where the point juts out
into the sea. Nobody's been there
for some time now. And let one try   30
the deep woods around Phyle, where
the wild boars so often charge
out of the brambles to wound shepherds
and gore cowherds. Let the pointers
free from their leads to run and catch
in silence whatever scent they can,
but keep the hounds and terriers close.
Soon enough, their time will come,
and hillsides will resound with belling
and baying, the blood aroused and calling   40
for hot blood of the quarry.
                                    Starting
early, we shall watch them quarter
the damp ground with noses twitching
and snuffling out whatever secrets

the earth keeps of what has passed by
in a darkness that is not quite gone.
    You've got your wide-meshed nets about you,
draped from your necks. You've got your snares
and the lead lines ready to stretch
from branches to frighten nervous deer   50
with bright feathers that hang in the air.
Startle and drive them into our blinds.
There, we shall lie in wait with curved
knives ready to flay their flesh
and carve and share delicious meat.
    O Diana, hunters' goddess,
be with us now, most gracious sovereign
over the world's woods as far
as the cold Araxes and clear-blue Ister.
We follow you as we follow only   60
the greatest gods, yielding our souls
to the grim transaction where you preside,
whether the fatal stroke is aimed
at noble lion, delicate deer,
stealthy tiger, shaggy bison,
or wild ox with its spreading horns.
Any hunter who follows the trail
of his chosen prey must learn to pray,
implore before, and, after, offer
thanks for a gift for which no man   70
ever feels quite worthy. Life
and death are your domain, and we
pay our homage to you as we lug
carcasses home on heavy wagons.
The dogs with their muzzles still red
from the gore of the kill look up to us
for approval, as we in turn look up
to you with thanks for your care. If our nets
held, it was only with your blessing;
if our spear points found accurate marks,   80
it was with your aid. O goddess, grant

again your favor. The dogs are baying,
and we prepare again to depart.
Good hunting, sirs.

(*Exit* HIPPOLYTUS *and* HUNTSMEN. *The light brightens on*
PHAEDRA, *who steps forward, followed by her* NURSE.)

PHAEDRA: Somewhere out there, beyond the horizon, Crete,
my island, rules the sea, her lovely vessels
plying the richest trade routes, but here I am,
her poorest daughter, given as hostage and bride
to Theseus, the man I hate. I spend
my days weeping; my nights are even worse,   90
whether I am assaulted or left alone
by a disrespectful husband who has taken off
on dangerous fool's errands with his crony,
his pal, Pirithoüs. They want to cross that river
no man returns from having crossed, and snatch
the queen of the underworld. A crazy project,
but at least it keeps him occupied while I
go crazy in other, sinister ways. A sickness
grows in my soul, and its heat fevers my blood
hotter and thicker than Etna's lava. I toss   100
on a sleepless bed, and pray in vain to Minerva
and deck her temples' altars with votive gifts,
but my torch gutters and smokes at her holy places.
My eyes have a will of their own and turn away
to Diana's groves and the beasts that run in the fields.
It's Pasiphaë's curse—the terrible call of the woods
to what we wouldn't otherwise even think of.
I recall my mother and what she must have suffered,
and feel her pains with my own—that unspeakable torment
of something that only wears love's clothing: obsession,   110
lust for a dream image that bounds into sight
in the waking world, turning it all to dream
and nightmare. She had to know it was crazy, could not
tear her eyes away from the beautiful beast
that glared back from his meadow, with a pure

black force she could not resist or ignore.
And I stare too, at another impossible object,
just as outrageous, and try to turn my head,
but my neck rejects my brain's command, and my eyes
are glued to him. Venus toys with us both,   120
demonstrating her majesty as if
we'd failed to acknowledge her deity's power. No
daughter of Minos has ever found her burden
easy to bear. My skin tingles with shame
and delight, and I am ashamed of that delight,
but nevertheless—or all the more—delighted.

NURSE: You must resist such thoughts. Do not give in,
but think instead of who you are—the queen,
and wife to Theseus, Jove's illustrious son!
These first subversive inklings you must stamp out   130
like small sparks struck from a flint, for the fire,
once it has caught and touched the heart's dry tinder,
can run wild and destroy you. The best defense
is the pride that comes from knowing who you are.
Second best is the shame you already feel,
even at having entertained the thought
of such transgressions. Only think where your mind
is leading your ignorant flesh! I know, I am old,
and it's easy, you think, for the old to be brave, who see
release at hand. To us, the exactions of tyrants   140
are temporary. But that's true for us all!
A lifetime, it turns out, is not such a huge
and unendurable span. What lasts is fame
and shame. Think of your mother's scandal! How
can you bring a new disgrace upon your house
and a further stain on its honor? Passion's a word
to make monstrous sin seem almost domestic,
or else to inflate it past all proportion. Fate
is not the grand *auteur* of these affairs:
they are merely errors of judgment, lapses of taste,   150
and failures of character, or they begin
that unimpressive way. What happens later

sometimes makes up in horror for what the squalid
first moments lacked in importance and stature.
Your husband is absent! Do you therefore suppose
yourself secure? You think to enjoy your guilt
in safety? It isn't merely Theseus' rage
you ought to fear but Minos', your father's fury.
He holds dominion over the hundred cities
and gives the laws to Crete—will he permit   160
his own daughter so great a crime? No secret,
however dark, can keep shame from the peering
eye of your mother's father—the Sun in Heaven,
who brings to light all manner of wickedness!
And he who makes the heavens quake, the father
of all the gods, will punish and cleanse those evils,
the offense of which ascends to foul his skies.

A distracted mind will invent excuses, reasons,
precedents—surely there must have been some women
who have managed to sin in safety, enjoyed themselves,   170
and have gone unpunished. Only poets and playwrights
suppose that every transgression produces the torments
their trade requires. Audiences expect it,
and the patrons want morality maintained—
you tell yourself, and hope it may be the truth.
There must be women who get away with mischief,
but who knows what they suffer when they're alone,
what torments conscience exacts from their souls? Recoil
from incestuous dreams that tempt you—father and son
sharing you, turning your womb to a sewer! It offends   180
nature, is monstrous. . . . Monsters have appeared,
and may again, to punish Cretan lusts.

PHAEDRA: What you say is true, but does no good at all.
I know what's good and what's bad. The abyss
is awful, and I look down and feel my knees
go weak. It's a fascination I hate! I'm drawn
like a sailor whose ship is caught in a strong tide
and fears the rocks but sees himself coming closer
moment by terrible moment, and nothing he does

can change his ruinous course! Passion's that tide   190
and the wingèd god is ruthless! Jove himself
has felt that power seize him, as Mars has been conquered,
Vulcan melted in flames hotter than Etna's,
and Phoebus' glory eclipsed by that naughty boy.

NURSE: I wonder who decided Love was a god.
Some lust-mad fool, I think it must have been,
or some seducer. Venus' impudent child
runs through the world making his innocent mischief
that's not so innocent after all, for he strikes
those few who are rich, healthy, already happy,   200
and ready thus to believe in happiness—almost
as if it were normal, as if we were all entitled
to be delighted, as if the whole point of our lives
were there, in the getting of pleasure, the taking or
  stealing. . . .
It's an elegant punishment, for feasts and parties
turn suddenly tame, the food and drink
lose all flavor. Propped on their pillows, sated,
they become their appetites, and nothing will serve
to satisfy their constant cravings for more,
and richer, and stranger, as their starving souls cry out   210
like those of piteous paupers. Control yourself,
or you are lost, and all you hold dear is lost.

PHAEDRA: That impish boy is as mighty as any god.
My husband will not come back. No man comes back
from that kingdom of darkness and silence. I'm certain of it!

NURSE: Nothing is ever certain. Theseus may
manage somehow to find a passageway back.

PHAEDRA: And such a hero may find a way to forgive me.

NURSE: He was severe when you were a virtuous wife,
  and your predecessor, Hippolyta, never found him   220
  tolerant or complaisant. Why would you think
  he has had some change of heart? And his son you ogle,
  is a pretty boy, I grant, but hardly a lover,
  or ladies' man. What makes you think he's eager,
  or willing, or even able? You've dreamed it all up
  out of nothing, or less than nothing, denying the truth
  of your eyes' and ears' reports. It's a sad delusion.

PHAEDRA: What's easy is never interesting. His charm—
  or part of it, surely—was in his elusiveness.
  Like the quarry he's always chasing, you hardly see him,   230
  except as a rustle of branches, a blur of feathers,
  or a glint in the water. You turn and stare, but he's gone,
  and there's only the space where he was, a moment ago,
  empty but lovely now for his having been there.

NURSE: You think you can catch him then? It's utter madness.
  There's no bait you can tempt him with. He's immune.
  And he's never liked you. You can't begin with friendship
  and work from there. It's you he chiefly despises,
  and, because of you, he avoids all womankind!

PHAEDRA: The wildest beast can be caught and tamed, with
    love.   240

NURSE: He'll bolt.

PHAEDRA: Let him run, or swim through the seas, or
                              fly,
  I'll catch him at last.

NURSE: Think of your father, Minos.

PHAEDRA: I think of my mother and what she dared to do.

NURSE: He avoids all women.

PHAEDRA: Then I shall have no rivals!

NURSE: Your husband will reappear!

PHAEDRA: With Pirithoüs!

NURSE: Your father may come.

PHAEDRA: Ariadne's father, too.
  He'll understand and forgive.

NURSE: By my white hairs,
  by my poor heart so worn with care, by my breasts
  on which you've lain your head, I beg you, woman,
  fight this madness. Take hold of yourself. To be cured,   250
  you must first wish to be well.

PHAEDRA: I am a queen
  and still know what shame is. I see what I'm doing.
  My hope is still that I may hold the tether
  of the wild beast my heart has become. It drags,
  but I am strong, and can fight it, even to death—
  which beckons. I could follow my husband down
  to the underworld, which offers a sure cure.

NURSE: Noble enough to die is noble enough
  to contrive a way to live. Restrain that mad
  passion of yours!

PHAEDRA: I am resolved on death.   260
  The only question is how I should meet my fate:
  with noose, or sharp swordpoint? Or shall I leap
  headlong from the parapet of the palace?

NURSE: Stop talking nonsense. You're posturing—I hope.
  It's not a gesture easily taken back.

PHAEDRA: It's not a gesture at all. One who's decided
that death is the only answer, the only right
solution to an impossible problem, is not
so easily deterred. It's a matter of honor.

NURSE: Nothing dire is required, for nothing will happen.   270
Your honor is safe. I'll even take your message,
so sure am I that stern young man will ignore us.

*(They exit into the palace. CHORUS enters, talking among them-
selves.)*

CHORUS: Goddess, born of the cruel sea,
who presides over loving and being loved,
and mother of that wanton boy
who shoots his arrows as if they were toys,
and plays with torches, delighting in flames
that destroy the lives of mortals, burning
souls and houses alike, to leave
ashes and ruin, goddess, spare us!   280

FIRST CHORISTER: They say one can feel the burning, slow
but moving along the veins and marrow,
so that one's own flesh turns hostile,
a traitor who throws open the gates
that protect what one has always valued—
treasure, honor, family, all
one had held dearest. Goddess, spare us!

SECOND CHORISTER: No one is safe. He roams the earth
from the lands in the east where the sun rises
to the shores in the west. North and south,   290
where nomads wander, he is at home,
striking sparks in the hearts of youths
and of old men, too, who know better
but rouse themselves to rejoin a disgraceful
dance they thought was over and done with.
The bosoms of shy maidens heave

with an unfamiliar heat. And the gods
themselves are not immune but descend
from high heaven, drawn to the dirt
and mud of earth. Goddess, spare us!   300

CHORUS: Jupiter turns himself into a swan,
  or into a bull, pawing the earth
  and breasting the waves for Europa's sake.
  There are many stories—Diana's mooning
  over Endymion, Hercules' labors
  for Omphale's sake. We tell them as marvels
  but feel fear, too, for their warning:
  at any improbable moment, passion
  can burst forth, an irrational longing
  to overthrow a settled existence,   310
  declaring how all that had gone before
  was worthless, trifling, merely illusion,
  but this, being new and strange, is real.

FIRST CHORISTER: They say that Hercules was so smitten
  as to dress himself like one of the women
  in Omphale's court. He would sit and spin
  but was clumsy holding the distaff, hopeless,
  so that the queen would slap her sandal
  upon his head and shoulders, wounding
  his hero's pride. Goddess, spare us!   320

CHORUS: Nowhere is safe, neither frozen tundra
  nor desert sands.
  Not even the depths of the sea are protected,
  but under the reef
  where the Nereids dwell, the arrows shimmer
  in cold current like eels and sting
  the water to burning.
  Not even the air, where the birds cavort,
  is thin enough,
  but the wingèd creatures suffer as we do.   330
  The fierce tiger in India's jungles

is harried and harries
just as the wild boar, goaded,
his terrible tusks
wet with the foam of his wanting, charges
in lust and madness from out of the brakes.

SECOND CHORISTER: Merciless, Amor drives them all,
and we, being weaker, try to outsmart
the cunning boy, but he scorns our efforts
and, teaching humility, strikes where he will   340
at the least likely, flaunting his power.

CHORUS: They say the lions in Africa roar
as if they're in pain
and the other fearful animals feel
at least for the moment some vindication.
Nothing is proof
against the god's mischievous whim.
We're in it together
and there's nothing to do but acknowledge our plight,
offer the goddess, his mother, our praise,   350
pray she be merciful, hope she may spare us!

FIRST CHORISTER: We know these things from our own lives and
        our friends'
erratic behavior. And there's never much to say
they won't resent later. Worse, there's the fear
of what the effect may be on our lives of the loves
of those in power, masters, noblemen, kings,
and queens who are driven to frenzy and recklessness,
which always spells ruin for those in the way.
(NURSE *reappears at the palace gateway*)
But, look, the nurse reappears. She will bring us news.
(*To* NURSE)
How is the queen? Those fires are raging still?   360

NURSE: Out of all control, she burns with fever.
  Her lips are shut, but her eyes betray her, glowing
  like hot coals. Her face is a silent scream,
  and her soul hides. She paces like some beast,
  restless and yet exhausted, about to collapse.
  She throws herself on her couch but cannot sleep,
  gets up, and walks a groove into the floor.
  Even her hair torments her. She puts it up,
  takes it down, brushes it, puts it up,
  as if there were living nerves on top of her head.   370
  Her clothing, too, displeases her, and she changes
  one robe for another, as if they were different
  selves she assumed, hoping for one she could bear.
  She takes no food or drink, as if she were warring
  with her own body, an enemy now. And she weeps,
  always weeps, for herself, for him, for the world
  in which such longing can happen and not be met
  with solace or satisfaction. Or say, she weeps
  for hope itself, which has abandoned her,
  or, worse, has died, leaving her and us   380
  to mourn together in endless obsequies.
  It breaks my heart to see it, but you may see
  for yourselves. The doors are opening. Look, my friends,
  at the poor dear, stricken, in pain on her couch.

(The doors are opened)

PHAEDRA: *(Distracted, almost crazed)*
  What to wear? I've nothing to wear! These clothes
  are dreary, drab. Gold, scarlet, and purple
  all turn tacky and boring. Jewelry's junk!
  What I want is a simple look, severe,
  with the clean lines of a hunting outfit. My hair
  should be falling down my neck like a dark cascade.   390
  No scent, either, but simple truth. And I'll hold
  a quiver and spear, for effect. And maybe a shield.
  Why not? A small shield! And I'll go to the woods
  to wander alone in the green silence and watch

how sunlight dapples down through the moving leaves.
I'll hear the songs of birds and see them fly,
and prove to myself that the natural world persists,
even with me in it. Or will it stop,
stricken, as I am stricken? Or merely offended?

FIRST CHORISTER: Take hold of yourself, my lady. To give in
    to grief   400
is never a cure. Pray to the goddess for strength.

NURSE: (*Praying*) O goddess of woods and groves, be with her
    now,
show her your loving kindness, grant her your gift.
Beyond all help but yours, she yearns for the beating
heart that soothes her own heart's pounding, his,
that boy of yours, that devoté who worships
in the glades that are your temples and altars, and groves
that are your colonnades. With your fine snares,
catch him as he catches scampering creatures,
soften his mind to her, and open his eyes   410
to the other life-and-death pursuit that ends
also with wild cries that are also prayers.
What you felt for Endymion she now feels
for her Hippolytus. Pity her mortal weakness,
and grant her your aid. Goddess of hills and meadows,
show us the gentled light of the new moon
that breaks through the tattered clouds to gleam and silvers
a dark hour with hope. Kindle that spark
in the heart of Hippolytus, and fan it into flames
that join the fire with which she burns. Sovereign   420
of night's secrets, preserve us another day,
another generation of men and women.
That youth who will not acknowledge his fealty needs
to be taught a lesson!
(HIPPOLYTUS *is seen approaching*)
                    But here he comes, prepared
to give thanks to the god for his hunt's success.
(*To herself*)

I must be bold, artful, and dare, for my mistress,
a crime I could not imagine, never mind
accomplish. She is my queen, and I therefore
owe her obedience. For us, in service, honor
is only a dream. We must content ourselves   430
if we can contrive for a while to avoid shame.

HIPPOLYTUS: What troubles you so? You seem upset? My father?
Phaedra? Their sons? They are all safe, I trust?

NURSE: There's nothing to fear on their account. It's you
I'm concerned about. For your sake am I distressed.
The way you've been living is wrong. It isn't healthy.
For some, it's fate that oppresses them, grief or illness
grinding them down. But you torment yourself.
You've got to learn to relax. Eat better. Drink—
yes, take a drink from time to time. They say   440
it's good for the system. Your life is passing you by
and, before you know it, your youth will be over. Gone!
Nothing but memories. . . . What will you remember?
What seems abstemious now will begin to look
crazy, stupid, and sinful. You now take pride
in how you deny yourself the trivial pleasures.
But what if you're wrong? What if they turn out to be
the whole point of life? You find that out
too late, and what can you do? In an open-minded
way you should at least try what you're missing.   450
A glass of wine. Or even a night with a woman.
    There's purpose in how we're made. The gods' intention
is perfectly clear. Sex is the answer to death,
or really the other side of the same coin,
and, devoting yourself as you do to hunting and fighting,
you have to recognize it's not just keeping the balance
but a deeper connection. They share the same excitement
and fascination, that sense they give of the real
business of living and dying. Devoted to one,
you're incomplete, only half a man. In time,   460
a boy must grow into manhood, take his place

in the long line of generations that link
the ages past with those that are yet to come.
Man is mortal, but, by the grace of Venus,
mankind can be immortal. Therefore, be humble
before the goddess of Love, who reigns over all
fleshly creatures. Look to the nature you love
and learn what the Fates demand. You are not exempt,
but must offer at last those sacrifices all
bodies imply—or pay the double debts   470
of Love and Death. You know what I say is true.
There is nothing wrong in the way you have lived thus far,
but to continue that way would be a mistake,
silly at first, and then ridiculous, then
an offense that seems less slight as time goes by
until, in the end, it is pride, a defiance of nature,
an affront to the gods. Your time in the woods is over.
Come into town, I pray you. Be a man.

HIPPOLYTUS: I am a man; my life is a manly one;
  I keep to the old ways. The paths I follow   480
  wind through the oldest forests, where air is clean
  and sharp with the tang of fir trees. The life of towns
  is corrupt, stinks. Nature can cleanse itself,
  but the foulness of civilization endures, persists,
  and spreads its poisons. The city's mob is a beast,
  or so they say—who never have know the wild
  and noble beasts they libel. Vermin, rather,
  noisy and smelly, surly, envious, mean,
  and faithless. *Honor* and *truth* are empty words   490
  in towns, but one may sometimes find, in the fields,
  some trace that they have been there, may still flourish,
  hidden in some glade. It's virtue I chase,
  and decency I hunt. My wants are simple,
  are those that any creature admits to. The wood
  can satisfy them all—a stream to drink from,
  nuts and berries to eat, and the starry sky
  over the bed I can make for myself of leaves
  and soft moss. A roof with a thousand pillars

holding it up is dangerous, can protect   500
from rain but leaves an occupant exposed
to worse threats—pride, for example, and fear
of envy in every quarter. Life in the woods
teaches a kinder lesson. The snares I set
are for beasts I kill for food. My bath is a clear
stream, and music I hear there isn't from slaves
but the songbirds in their freedom, just as the dance
is that of light and shadow, the dapple of leaves
the breezes stir. To learn to enjoy such gifts
is to know a contentment far more secure than wealth   510
can ever offer. To rely on one's own skill
and speed and catch one's own dinner is freedom,
a power greater than any that's still beholden
to mobs' moods or armies' or kings' whims.
Who lies on grass, surrounded by budding flowers,
enjoys wealth he knows he must lose, for flowers
wilt and die. Such momentary pleasures
can teach us to give thanks but not hold on
too tightly, a trick only noble souls
can master. Luxury softens, corrupts, and gold   520
cups poison whatever refreshing drink
touches the vessels' metal. In golden ages,
nobody hoards gold, and the bountiful earth
is not disfigured with boundary stones and fences.
Cities were not surrounded by curtain walls
set with fortified towers. Men did not study
the weapons of warfare that greed and fear enforce
on victim and victimizer, deforming the lives
of both. I hunt in the woods for a better idea
of what life may be like, and ask for nothing   530
beyond the bare subsistence my body needs.
I hate the city. Even the farmer's life
seems to me oppressive—he yokes his oxen
and turns the guiltless animals into slaves
to scratch at the earth for a livelihood that reeks
of toil and sweat. I flee from that to the woods,
where we all lived before the desires for wealth

and power turned mankind wicked or crazy.
Some small hoard of food must have begun it—
some lazy villain thought to steal, and they fought,   540
hand to hand, and then with stones and clubs,
and then with iron-tipped spears, then swords and helmets,
to take what this man has, or keep that man
from taking what you've amassed. All civilization—
which everyone seems so proud of—is bathed in blood,
rivers of blood from piteous, countless wounded.
Brother dispatches brother, and fathers kill
their own sons. Husbands die, and the weapons
drip gore on the hands of the wives who struck them
the deadly blows. Jealousy, envy, madness   550
possess a mind, and mothers kill their children
in crimes that outrage Nature and make her shudder.
And I'm not speaking of stepmothers: we know
what they are capable of, how little children
suffer hurts that turn them vicious, crazy,
and worse than any beasts. What women do
in darkened rooms of the houses on any street
of any town would set a stone to weeping.
Cruelty, envy, and lust, arising like smoke
from their cooking fires, sting the eyes of men,   560
and cities burn, and kingdoms are overthrown.
As children, we learn the stories. One needn't rehearse
all the terrible names. But think of Medea.
And she's not alone: all women bring destruction.

NURSE: For the crimes of only a few, you blame us all?

HIPPOLYTUS: I detest you all, and fear and shun and curse you
    all. From reason, or instinct, or in a rage
    that does not admit of explanation, I hate
    and despise all womankind, without exception!
    Sooner shall fire and water mingle; sooner   570
    shall ships find haven among the shifting Syrtes'
    sandbanks; sooner shall we look out to westward

to watch the dawn break; sooner shall hungry wolves
gaze with solicitude upon grazing deer
than my detestation of women will subside.

NURSE: Love can gentle the stubborn heart and soften
obdurate hatred—even yours. Your mother's
Amazon sisters killed male children, but spared
one, as you bear witness, willing or not.

HIPPOLYTUS: One solace for Mother's death is that my
    hatred   580
of the female gender now can be universal.

NURSE: As waves on the black rocks break into spray
and disappear, my words on his skull shatter.
(*She turns to the palace and sees* PHAEDRA)
But the queen comes, Phaedra, and in some hurry.
Where will luck and her own madness lead her?
(PHAEDRA *staggers down the steps, lurches, and falls.*
   HIPPOLYTUS *goes to her and raises her head in his arms.*)
Fainted, is she? But pallor is hard to fake.
Perhaps she has. Wake! Hippolytus holds you.

PHAEDRA: Who brings me back to consciousness and grief?
There was, for a moment, relief, a blessèd release.

HIPPOLYTUS: How can you speak so of the gift of life?   590

PHAEDRA: (*Aside*) Be bold, my soul, and dare to ask for the gift
you long to possess. Silence is unrewarding,
and I may as well admit that the sin of loving
is established now, committed. The time for shame
is long past. One may as well go forward
in the hope of some success that could sanctify
this scandal. We look at marriages all around us,
with no idea of the anguish in which they began,
or perhaps remember the rumors, once disgraceful

but now a kind of joke. I must have faith.   600
(*To* HIPPOLYTUS)
I pray you, let us speak for a time in private.

HIPPOLYTUS: Speak, by all means. There's nobody here.

PHAEDRA: Speak . . . I wish I could. The words don't come.
I wish to speak, but lack the will. My lips
and tongue can scarcely move, and my throat is tight.

HIPPOLYTUS: Your heart desires something it cannot name?

PHAEDRA: Dares not. Only trivial troubles babble.

HIPPOLYTUS: I pray you, mother, trust, confide in me.

PHAEDRA: Mother! That name is a proud title I don't
deserve or want. Call me anything else—   610
sister, or even slave. Yes, slave will do,
for I should adore to serve, to walk behind you
even barefoot, even through deep snowdrifts.
I am your captive and, captivated, live
only to demonstrate total devotion. Bid me
walk through flames and I shall go most gaily
into the fire. Send me into battle,
and I shall be happy to offer my breast to the naked
swords of your foes. Only express a wish
and I shall obey, for you are now my master.   620
Hold out your arms to your suppliant and pity
a widow's abject surrender.

HIPPOLYTUS: Surely, not so!
My father will soon return, alive and in health.

PHAEDRA: Who has ever recrossed the Styx? Those waters
are dark and deep: no one returns to the brightness
that lights our upper world. He and his friend

will never make Pluto a laughingstock, can never
come back to us here.

HIPPOLYTUS: The kindly gods will bring him
   back to us both and my brothers, too. Meanwhile,
   I shall be willing to serve as his regent, sharing   630
   your burdens—but you must not think yourself widowed.

PHAEDRA: (*Aside*) He refuses to understand? I must be more
   plain,
   and spell it all out as if he were still a child.
   (*To* HIPPOLYTUS)
   Have pity on me, I pray, and hear what I say,
   although I blush to pronounce what I yearn to speak.

HIPPOLYTUS: Madam, I don't understand you. What is the
   matter?

PHAEDRA: A matter most unmaternal, or step-maternal,
   and therefore hard to believe.

HIPPOLYTUS: And the matter is?
   You speak in riddles! Tell me, in simple words!

PHAEDRA: Love! Is that simple enough? Do you
   understand?   640
   I burn with love! Driven to madness, I suffer
   terrible torments, as if my veins were on fire.

HIPPOLYTUS: Yes, in love. With Theseus, my father!

PHAEDRA: No, Hippolytus, listen to me. I love
   Theseus' face as it used to be, his youthful
   face before that heavy beard grew in.
   His body, when he was young, was a wonder, smooth
   skin over the long muscles, his arms
   and legs strong, yes, but still gorgeous.
   He knew how good he looked, and it bothered him, too: 650

he blushed a lot, as young girls often do.
One's heart trembled to see him, as mine does still
when it sees those features, those same looks and blushes,
the same muscled body and smooth skin
your father used to have alive in you.
I see that beauty replicated or even
surpassed, for you have something of your mother's
severe good looks. It's rather as though a Greek
artist had redone a Scythian statue
and given its simple energy a finesse   660
that only made it stronger. If, to Crete,
you and he had come to our shores together,
it's you we should have chosen. Ariadne,
my sister, fell in love with him and, abandoned,
hanged herself, but still in love. He ruined
her, but now it's you who have ruined me.
(*She kneels to* HIPPOLYTUS)
I am a king's daughter and kneel before you
to humble myself in prayer. I beg your pity—
for yours is the power now. Help me, and end
the pain one way or the other: indulge my longing   670
or else snuff out my unbearable life.

HIPPOLYTUS: What?
Can the gods hear this and not cry out? The skies
are clear that should rage with thunder and lightning. Clouds
should hide the light of a mortified sun, ashamed
at this obscene suggestion! Stars should writhe
out of their normal courses, deranged by this
violation of nature's most basic laws.
Jupiter, ruler of gods and men, should hurl
cleansing thunderbolts to burn corruption
pure again, if any such thing exists   680
as purity in this world. But how would I know,
infected as I am, corrupted myself
as I must be, having provoked such a thing
as my stepmother's lewd suggestion?
(*To* PHAEDRA)

I beg
pardon, but what have I done to invite what you
propose, or suggest it's thinkable? What crimes
are imputed to me that lead the world to suppose
there's nothing I wouldn't stoop to? Has my whole life
been a charade, a mistake? I've lived austerely
and disdained the trite temptations of the flesh,   690
but you haven't noticed. Or lust has you hypnotized,
entranced so you sleepwalk through a nightmare world
more monstrous than your own mother's issue.
The Minotaur wasn't so much a freak as you,
for his deformities were all overt, while yours,
as hideous as his, are hidden away
behind a façade that does not arouse one's fear
and appropriate loathing. We have not, in this house,
fared well with our stepmothers. My father's
stepmother was Medea: she tried to kill him.   700
I envy him now, having myself a viler
and crazier one than he ever had to suffer.

PHAEDRA: You're right. I am not myself. My house is cursed:
we want what we know we ought to abhor, but still
crazily crave. Wherever you flee, I'll follow,
utterly shameless, lost. I kneel before you.

(*She kneels and seizes his hand*)

HIPPOLYTUS: (*Recoiling*) No! Don't touch me! Vile woman! Vile
and shameless. . . . The only purification is blood
that must be spilled . . .
(*He draws his sword*)
                    O Diana, bless me!

PHAEDRA: Do it. Thrust! Heal me of my madness!   710
To die by your dear hand would be welcome, lovely!

(*She grabs the sword and places it at her breast*)

HIPPOLYTUS: (*He flings away the sword*)
   Disgusting! Loathsome! Your touch pollutes my blade.
   I'm tainted. I feel filthy. No sea can wash
   this foulness from me. Away, into the woods!

(*He rushes off and into the forest*)

NURSE: (*To the audience*)
   Her sin is revealed. How can I bear it in silence?
   What can I do to help her? That prissy boy
   must somehow be made to suffer as she has suffered.
   All that smug outrage was unnecessary.
   He even enjoyed himself. But we shall see
   how he likes having the tables turned. In the wrong,   720
   one should always attack. To do nothing is fatal.
   (*She tears* PHAEDRA's *dress and musses her hair. Then to the*
      wings.)
   Help! Athenians, help! Rape! Rape!
   Come to our aid! That wicked boy is crazy!
   Mad with lust and shameless, he threatens his queen
   and stepmother and then, a coward, flees!
   After him! Catch him! Bring him back to justice!
   (*Two* SERVANTS *appear*)
   See, he has left his sword. He threatened to kill her
   if she would not let him have his nasty way.
   She struggled and cried out! Look at her hair,
   her torn clothing. Oh, the pig! The monster!   730
   Attend to the queen. Bear her into the palace.
   (*To* PHAEDRA)
   Poor dear! It will be fine. You'll see.
   You're safe now. Nobody blames you. No one!
   Don't say a word. You're among your friends and safe.
   It's a bad dream you've had, but it's over now.

(*They exit.* CHORUS *convenes to discuss these events.*)

FIRST CHORISTER: He was out of here, like a meteor's tail,
    gone in a blur. One rubbed one's eyes
    in doubt of their report, and stars
    danced in the darkness.
    A handsome fellow, a perfect model   740
    of what a man ought to look like: the gods
    envy such looks and exact payment
    from those so blessed.
    The gift of beauty becomes a curse,
    as the mind, reeling, tries to establish
    what to expect, what is deserved,
    or what is the cost.
    Beauty at any rate fades away,
    having been only briefly enjoyed,
    and leaves the spirit impoverished, crazed.   750
    What can it mean?

SECOND CHORISTER: It happens in nature: a meadow blooms
    rich with flowers, and twittering birds
    celebrate the place and the moment
    that quickly fades,
    and the meadow is merely a fallow field,
    a tangle of weeds that cannot remember
    how, in the spring, for a day or two
    a dream touched it,
    and then moved on. Flowers in fields   760
    and those in the cheeks of youths and maidens
    can blossom to make a passing stranger
    gasp in amazement,
    but also in grief, for we know what will happen,
    sooner than later. All flowers fade,
    and the gift of their presence is taken away.
    It's a terrible lesson.
    Not even the wise can claim they've achieved
    the delicate balance we need to enjoy
    without holding on too tightly to beauty   770
    we glimpse or exhibit.

FIRST CHORISTER: Being immortal, the gods can rely
    on expanses of time. The same good looks
    in a mortal man or woman have barbs
    cruel as a fishhook's.
    For us, time's abrasions disfigure
    the face, bleach the hair, corrode
    the skin, and cause the belly to sag.
    We become grotesques
    of earlier selves and see in the glass   780
    only burlesque, unkindness, unlikeness.
    Nowhere is safe. In the grand salons
    catty remarks
    that sooner or later you overhear
    will let you know the truth you've almost
    evaded, avoided, or tried to ignore.
    But out in the country,
    the same thing happens, a cruel declension
    from godlike looks to more and more
    earthly versions, imperfect copies,   790
    wind-roughened,
    sun-toughened, and crude and coarse.
    It always happens, and still it always
    is unexpected and takes unawares
    the otherwise clever
    and circumspect man or woman, as death
    seems to sneak up. We supposed there might
    be an exception from time to time,
    but no such luck.

SECOND CHORISTER: Brute strength avails nothing,   800
    for even the strongest lose their power,
    little by little, and one who could pass
    as a Hercules
    or warlike Mars diminishes, tamed
    by time's assaults, or its cowardly backstabs.
    Therefore, learn to live in the moment,
    enjoying as gift
    what you realize is only on loan.

Ride out on horseback, shooting your arrows
into the sky at birds on the wing,   810
and feeling the wind
in your hair, on your face, in your innermost soul,
and share the ascent of the shaft from your quiver,
but marking as well the parabola's other
descending side,
an unvarying answer we never quite master,
however frequent its demonstration.
We think we are safe as the birds in a cloud,
and then out of nowhere
that arrow appears to correct, disabuse us.   820
And if the sharp point were not wounding enough,
our bitter chagrin would be ample to bring us
abruptly to earth.

FIRST CHORISTER: Still, having said all that, we must get down to
      cases.
    What the woman is trying to do is outrageous. The boy
    is guiltless. She is the guilty one. And justice
    must always prevail.

SECOND CHORISTER: Must it? You really think so?
    She weeps. Her hair is disheveled. She uses the arts
    women have that often work.

FIRST CHORISTER: Hold on.
    Someone is coming, noble or even royal—   830
    to judge from the way he carries himself. But pale,
    as if recovered from illness.

SECOND CHORISTER: It is the king,
    Theseus himself, restored to the light.
    (THESEUS enters, accompanied by two SERVANTS)
    We welcome you, sire, and pray you tell us your story.

THESEUS: I have escaped at last from the realm of night,
    the prison of shades and shadows, the land of death.
    My eyes can hardly endure the daylight's dazzle.
    Two years have elapsed since I have been dangling over
    the deepest abyss there is, that chasm of darkness
    into which we all plunge sooner or later.   840
    I was dead to pleasure, friendship, love, to all
    but rage at injustice. To that I clung, and by that,
    and with Hercules' strength and aid, dragged myself back
    and up to rejoin, at least for a while, the world.
    To Hercules I owe my deliverance, spent
    and weak as I am, a shadow of my old self
    and only half-alive, for my soul is sick,
    sick unto death.
    (A woman's cry is heard)
                But what is that cry?
    What grief, what outrage waits to assault my spirit,
    a bruise on a bruise? Speak! Tell me the dire   850
    news I shall soon enough hear and, somehow, endure,
    the only right welcome for one who returns
    from Phlegethon and torment's infernal kingdom.

(NURSE enters, distraught)

NURSE: My mistress scorns our tears, is deaf to our pleading,
    and Phaedra's iron purpose now is death.

THESEUS: But why? And why now? I have come back alive!

NURSE: That is precisely the cause for her wish to die.

THESEUS: You're speaking in riddles. Tell me plainly. Explain
    what grief now weighs on her spirit. Say what has happened.

NURSE: She will not disclose it. She sorrows but will not   860
    speak. All she says is that she will take
    to the grave her terrible secret, the shame of which
    will be buried with her. But you must help her. Hurry!

THESEUS: (*To* SERVANTS)
   Open the portals wide.
   (*They do so, revealing* PHAEDRA, *reclining on a couch, holding
      a sword*)
                              Phaedra, what is it?
Is this how you welcome your lord's return? Your husband
greets you again, and you turn away from him
and from life itself! Put up that sword, and speak
so that I may put right whatever has gone so wrong.

PHAEDRA: Alas, Theseus, I beg you by all you hold dear—
   your kingdom's scepter, your children, my body, allow me   870
   to go where you have come from.

THESEUS: Why should you die?

PHAEDRA: To speak the reason would be to defeat it.

THESEUS: I swear,
   no other ears but mine shall hear what you say.

PHAEDRA: But yours are the only ears I fear to dirty
   with this vile tale.

THESEUS: I'll bury it in my heart.

PHAEDRA: It would corrupt it. Let me die!

THESEUS: By force
   I can take that sword away from you.

PHAEDRA: But cunning
   can conquer force. Death is not hard to arrange.

THESEUS: Tell me what crime it is you wish to expunge.

PHAEDRA: That I am alive is a crime.

THESEUS: Do my tears not move
                                        you?   880

PHAEDRA: I love them, and to die with your tears' balm
  is my last wish.

THESEUS: (*To his* SERVANTS *and* CHORUS)
  More faithful, is she, to silence than to me?
  There are ways, admittedly crude, to discover the truth,
  nevertheless.
  (*To* SERVANTS)
                        Have the old nurse bound
  hand and foot. Bring out the whips. We'll drag
  the secret out, whatever it is, I promise.

PHAEDRA: No, don't. Don't. I will confess.

THESEUS: I supposed
  you'd see the light. But why do you weep? Trust me!
  Only speak and I'll do what I can, I promise.

PHAEDRA: (*After a pause, looking heavenward*)
  O Jupiter, lord of the gods, I call   890
  on you as witness, and you, lord of the sun
  and founder of this house, in both your names . . .
  (*To* THESEUS)
  I fought him off. I withstood his pleading, his threats.
  My honor and yours have not been stained, I swear,
  although my body suffered his violent assault.
  My blood shall wash all shame of it away.

THESEUS: Not your blood; his! But who did this? Name him!

PHAEDRA: Whom you'd least suspect!

THESEUS: Stop playing games.
  The name!

PHAEDRA: His sword will tell what I dread to pronounce. He left
    it,
fleeing in terror and shame, as the citizens came   900
in answer to my cries. You'll recognize it.

THESEUS: (*Examining the sword*)
    No!
    (*Softer, in grief*)
        No. What monstrous thing is this?
I know this sword, this hilt, this royal seal
of Athens, the device of my own house.
But where has he gone?

PHAEDRA: The slaves here saw him flee
    into those woods he knows so well to hide.

THESEUS: What kind of son is this? He is a throwback,
    nurtured by Greece, but wild, that Scythian stock
    blooming again, debased, some savage primate.
    But that's not fair to the beasts whom instinct teaches   910
    to avoid the sin of incest. Was it all just sham,
    that show of virtue and strenuous chastity?
    What has become of us? What kind of age is this
    when such outrage can walk among us, smile,
    and assume that the smiling faces of others conceal
    at least a like depravity? False men
    walk in the streets, sit at our tables, and talk,
    mouthing pieties, turning them into a joke
    nobody laughs at. Decency now is the costume
    indecency wears, as brashness pretends to be meek,   920
    and indolence gets itself up to look like zeal.
    One's stomach turns. . . .
                    He said he loved the woods,
believed in the simple and modest life. He despised
the town and its misdemeanors, keeping himself
as a chaste bridegroom for his bridal bed for this
felony, this sin against his father,
nature, and the gods, whom I now thank

for having let me strike down Hippolyta,
his mother, with my own hand. I should have killed
him, too. Him first. A fugitive, he will wander   930
the earth as a stranger, all men's hands against him.
Let him explore the snows of the north, the dry
deserts of the south, the eastern steppes,
the western oceans, and find no hiding place
for such an offense. His infamy will precede him
into trackless wastes where primitive tribes squat
around their cooking fire. They will shun him.
And always behind him, relentless, I shall follow,
into the farthest regions of earth, hurling
furious curses upon him and prayers and, at last,   940
my weapons as well.
                              Neptune, lord of the sea,
granted me three prayers I could make in his name
that the gods would grant, and swore by the mighty Styx
a binding oath. I call upon him now.
(*To Neptune*)
Great lord of the sea, O father, hear me,
and grant me this last of the favors I beg and claim
as part of your gift. Let Hippolytus die.
Let him enjoy the light of the sun no more.
Let him be cut down in the day of his youth,
and let him join those ghosts I have just encountered   950
who hate me still, and let them extract from him
their worst and fondest vengeance. This I ask.
Enjoying this gift of yours, I was no mere mortal
but like a god; I use now my last prayer.
In the bitterness of my heart, I descend to mere
manhood again, and am content. But hear me,
make your waves crash on rocks in fury,
and spit rage that blows the stars from the sky.

CHORUS: Mother Nature, Father God,
      how decorous the order of your sky.   960
      Why does it mock us?
      The planets wheel, and the constellations turn

unswerving and just
over an earth that is soaked in blood
and reels from injustice.
You give us a vision of order and peace,
and the cold winds blast it,
or the heat of the summer bakes, and it shrivels and dies.
The wheels of ponderous engines turn in the heavens,
and a stately music arises, but here on earth   970
dissonant cries of victims resound.
How can you show us your face but from such a distance?
You prove your existence but then ignore our prayers
and turn your faces away from the piteous wounds
generations have borne.
Evil goes unpunished; good, unrewarded.
We call out like children
calling to parents they need and love, but the answer
is silence or, worse, the mocking and empty wind
blowing on desolate rocks.   980
Villains rule us, and fools are given honor,
while virtue weeps and is scorned. And you permit this?
What can your purpose be? The stars in their courses
tease and torment us, insult us, commanding our love,
but their fair promises all prove cruel and false
and utterly empty.

FIRST CHORISTER: We only say what everyone says. We speak
    the bitter truth that lies in each man's heart
    if only he's brave or desperate enough to admit it.

SECOND CHORISTER: I'm afraid you're right. But look,
        someone is coming,   990
    a messenger, out of breath, his face tear-stained.

(*Enter* MESSENGER)

MESSENGER: It could have been anyone. I was unlucky and drew
    the short straw. I come with terrible news.

THESEUS: Whatever it is, speak out. You've nothing to fear.
  Our expectations are bad enough. We are ready.

MESSENGER: I can scarcely get out the words for the grief I feel.

THESEUS: Do not presume above your station but speak!

MESSENGER: It is most lamentable, sire. Your son is dead.

THESEUS: In my heart, my son was already dead. You bring
  news of the end of a would-be rapist. Tell us.   1000

MESSENGER: He had fled on foot at first but made for the stables,
  where he hitched his horses, the matched chestnut pair
  to the light chariot, and all the time he cursed
  fate and native country, and yet he called
  upon you, his father, for justice. He departed
  in a thunder of hoofbeats, taking the shore road,
  and lashing the backs of the beasts. The sea was quiet,
  a glassy blue, and the winds were all but calm,
  the fishermen say, as Hippolytus went past them,
  but then, out of nowhere, out of the sea's cold depths,   1010
  a violent storm arose, a waterspout
  with enormous waves that broke on the rocks, grasping,
  even vindictive. . . . A marvel! A dreadful thing.
     On the boats still out, there was panic. Some overturned,
  but not even those on shore felt safe. The water
  clawed at the jetties, the cliffs, the pier's pilings,
  as if to sweep the whole beach clean and destroy
  not only those who have made their living at sea,
  but those inland who have never been in a boat.
  Walls of water came rushing in. Whole houses   1020
  turned into flotsam and drifted away. The sacred
  Epidauran boulders of Aesculapius
  were totally covered, which no one can remember
  having happened before. The isthmus was all submerged,
  and the Peloponnese was an island, wholly cut off.
  We worried it wouldn't stop, that the surge of water

would just keep coming, would swallow all dry land
everywhere, that the end of the world had come,
that mountains would be submerged, that the fish would take
   over
the universe. We assumed we were going to die   1030
and had given up all hope but were yet appalled
by what we saw, for out of the churning waters
we saw a monster, a terrible creature, a whale,
but larger than any whale, with a towering neck
and a kind of mane that gave it a warlike look,
and ears and horns, and eyes that burned with fire,
now red, now reddish purple, now orange-gold.
A sea creature, it nevertheless breathed air,
and we saw how its nostrils flared, greedy, enraged,
in stertorous gasps of what we were sure was fury.   1040
    To drown is bad enough, and we've learned to live
under that threat, who live on the sea. But this,
this creature, this monstrous thing, was something worse. . . .
To be torn apart, mangled, and maybe eaten,
to go at last in some agonizing way
no one has ever expected or thought to fear
was awful. Our marrow froze and our very souls,
and not just men, but the grazing cattle were frightened,
bolted, and ran, even milch cows stampeding.
The goats ran, and the sheep on the mountainsides   1050
bleated and ran.
             But Hippolytus stood his ground,
unafraid, and held his team tight-reined,
crooning and calming his terrified steeds. Amazing,
as horrified as we were, to see his courage
in the face of that brutal specter, but, undismayed,
he held his horses steady, although he knew
it had come for him, the sudden storm, the bull-like
creature from out of the sea. There is a meadow
where sea grasses wave, flat between the hills,
and there it had come ashore, not dragging itself   1060
but running, fleet of foot, scarce deigning to touch
the caked sand of the beach. It darted, feinted,

and then it charged, roaring in frenzy and spite.
The horses screamed in terror, but your son was fearless,
never once quailed, but addressed the beast in defiance:
"My father has tamed such bulls as you. Our line
does not give way to the bellow of empty threats.
Stand and fight!"
                But his own horses betrayed him.
In panic, they bolted, lunging out of control.
No man could have held them, for terror lashed   1070
an unbearable whip. They broke and ran, and your son
had all he could do to keep from being thrown
as the chariot bounced and caromed over the marsh
and among the rocks. An astonishing feat it was,
but he held on somehow, as they ran straight on
as if they were charging the beast from the sea, but they
   turned,
suddenly swerving, wrenching their necks in the yoke,
and the chariot tipped, and Hippolytus fell, entangled
and struggling in the reins to get himself free,
but the more he struggled, the tighter he seemed bound, 1080
and the horses now ran uncontrolled as panic
drove them faster. He bounced on the ground, was dragged,
trying to miss the rocks, but helpless, bruised,
battered, terribly bloodied. The path they made
was blazed in blood. And then, abruptly, they stopped,
where the stump of a tree, like a stake planted in warfare,
speared him through, impaling his groin, and holding
Hippolytus, horses, and overturned chariot, all. . . .
Awful, and then they broke, broke free, broke him.
I think it was over then, he could not have felt   1090
what happened after. The horses plunging and running,
dragging the body behind them, or what remained
that hadn't caught on the thorns, bushes, rocks,
and brambles. That lovely face was gone, that perfect
beauty now obliterated, defiled,
its memory only underscoring the horror
of what we tried to turn our eyes away from
but could not, held by the horror, caught as he

had been caught himself.
                     The horses stopped at last,
and it was over. We walked as in a nightmare,   1100
to gather up the bits of his broken body
that we could find for the funeral pyre or followed
where dogs, whimpering, pointed. Most of the corpse
we think we recovered. But how can one know? To inspect
the gory fragments requires a stronger stomach
and harder heart than anyone of our village
can even imagine. The ruin of Phaëthon's car
when the sun's horses ran wild was hardly worse
than this woeful carnage through which we picked our way.
Bits and bloody pieces, droplets of gore,   1110
and a smear of brains. . . .

(SERVANTS *enter, bearing a box with the pieces of Hippolytus in it.*
They set it down before THESEUS.)

THESEUS: My son, my poor son!
Guilty, I wished him dead, but now I lament,
even against my will. O my poor boy.
How could it come to this?

MESSENGER: How can you weep
for answered prayers? What you willed has happened.
You can't have it both ways.

THESEUS: I weep the worse
and bitterer tears: I hate what I had to pray for.

MESSENGER: Does the weeping mean your hatred at last is
    ended?

THESEUS: I weep that I had to kill the son I loved.
I weep for myself and perhaps weep for a world   1120
in which such vile and unspeakable things can happen.

FIRST CHORISTER: How does Fortune toy with us all!
   The high and mighty dashed down like playthings
   of naughty children. We who are more obscure
      are also safer.

SECOND CHORISTER: The storms rage at the peaks of mountains,
   but lower down the bite of the winds
   is less keen, and the lightning bolts
      rarely strike.

FIRST CHORISTER: Sometimes it seems like spite, that the
     rich,   1130
   powerful, handsome, or happy are picked
   and made to suffer, an object lesson
      to keep us humble . . .

SECOND CHORISTER: As if the gods were jealous, as if
   they hated for men to enjoy the gifts
   immortals would rather retain for themselves,
      as if they were mean.

FIRST CHORISTER: But who could believe in such beings or
     worship
   except to appease malevolent beings?
   I cannot believe it. I refuse to accept it.   1140
      And yet there he is.

   (*Indicating* THESEUS)

FIRST CHORISTER: Back from the dead, the king of Athens,
   almost a god himself, is struck down
   in what should have been his moment of triumph,
      is the saddest of men.

SECOND CHORISTER: If I were he, I'd long to go back
   to the land of the dead, where these vivid events
   might pale in the shadows, and where I could weep
      hidden in darkness.

CHORUS: Pallas Athena, goddess who keeps our city   1150
   secure and protects us, show us thy mercy, we pray,
   and spare our noble king any further torments.
   The father escaped from the land of the dead, but the son,
   Hippolytus, has gone down to fill that place.

(*A woman's wail is heard*)

FIRST CHORISTER: What sound is that? What further grief can
   befall us?

SECOND CHORISTER: It's Phædra, disheveled, and bearing a
   naked sword.

(PHAEDRA *enters, sword in hand, and moaning*)

THESEUS: Still carrying on? But why the sword?
   Is there something else, something I don't yet know?
   Why this lamentation over his corpse?

PHAEDRA: I should be there, dead, broken in pieces.   1160
   The monster that Neptune sent should have come for me.
   It would have been kinder. Perhaps I shall go to him,
   wading into the waves, deeper and deeper.
   O Theseus, you are so good a man,
   but those around you suffer. Hippolyta dead,
   and now her son dead, too. But I still live. . . .
   Isn't it most peculiar, don't you think?
   (*She turns to address the mangled corpse*)
   Where is your terrible beauty now? Poor boy!
   Is that what became of you, who were so becoming,
   so impossibly gorgeous . . . I'll make it up.   1170
   If you have a spirit that hears me, listen! I promise,
   what I promised before. You ran away from me then;
   you can't run now. But I may contrive to follow
   at a slow pace, wade through Styx's waters,
   saunter through burning fires, pursuing you still,
   as I said I would. We never were joined in life,

but life isn't all there is—and death allows us
the impossible things we can't bear life without.
Here, we mingle already . . .
(*She cuts a lock of hair from her head and drops it into the
    coffin*)
                              and are joined in death.
But how does the rest of me stand? How can I face   1180
my husband now? Or go to his bed, defiling
it, him, myself, that poor dead body.
That would be worse than what has gone before,
corruption upon corruption. Better to die,
for solace, penance, forgiveness, a kind of cleansing.
I come to my death as my last and only hope
and fly to its open and welcoming arms.
(*To* THESEUS *and* CHORUS)
                                    Hear me,
Athens, and you, his father and our king,
hear me confess my crimes. I have lied to you all.
I was crazy with lust for the beautiful boy and helpless,   1190
and my charge against him was false. Utterly false!
Your punishment was wrong. He had done nothing.
He fled from me in horror, was utterly chaste
and noble and good. Which was why I loved him so.
Beautiful, noble, and good. And look what it came to. . . .
Ruined, broken in bits.
(*To the corpse*)
                          But now your honor
is put together again. I have set that right.
And my blood shall atone for the blood you shed,
if blood can atone for blood. But what else can?
(*To* THESEUS)
I beg your pardon. I beg everyone's pardon.   1200
Perhaps I shall soon see all of you in hell.

(*She falls on her sword and dies*)

THESEUS: I have crossed the stinking lake of Avernus, have seen
those stagnant pools of Lethe that welcome her now,
and I long to have their gift of forgetfulness.
If I had one more prayer, I'd ask for that monster
to come back for me too, bearing me off
and delivering me from pain. I cannot command,
but still can beg. O father, hear me, grant
that extra favor, having fulfilled so swiftly
the last of my three wishes. Your poor grandson   1210
is dead. And your son's heart is filled with grief
and the bitter gall of knowing that I was wrong,
judged too quickly, sinned against my own
flesh and house. He was innocent: I
am the guilty one and deserve to suffer as he
has already suffered. Hercules brought me forth
from the land of the dead. I wish now to return
for good, or at least forever. To disappear.
What I most regret is ever having been born.
I have offended heaven, insulted hell,   1220
and polluted the ocean. Thrice accursed I am,
and hate myself as any man would hate
the villain of such tales as have been my story.
    Did I come back for this? Was my life so fine
as to need renewal? I yearned for the light of the sun,
but what it has shown me is murder and suicide.
With a single torch I can set both pyres aflame.
Widowed, childless, I cannot turn to a friend
for sympathy, having myself caused one and then
the other to die, nor look for any vengeance   1230
except in a glass. Hercules, take me back
into the deepest shadows of unbeing
where the stern judges wait who contemplate evil
and devise bizarre and proportionate torments for villains.
Shall I be tied between two bent pine trees
that will tear me in half as Sciris used to do?
Or thrown from a cliff as Sciron did to his victims?
Or plunged into pools of Lethe? Or Phlegethon's fires?
Something awful, exquisite, eternal . . .

I cannot think what it might be. Sisyphus,   1240
Tantalus, Ixion, all together, their torments
somehow combined. I came last time as a thief;
this time I come as a suppliant, follow my son,
and only ask the punishment I deserve
from any plausible gods.

FIRST CHORISTER: Your lamentations
   may never end. Now, you must bury your son,
   whatever there is, as much of him as they've found.

THESEUS: Bring the remains hither. Whatever is left,
   let it be piled together that I may atone
   for my injustice. I, having wished him dead,   1250
   must force myself to gaze upon this horror.
   (SERVANTS *file in, carrying small containers*)
   I beg my father's pardon, having commanded
   a terrible thing. I behold his awful gift,
   childless—as he must also now wish himself.
      Is this what is left of my son? My wicked heart
   breaks to see it.

FIRST CHORISTER: This is his right hand.

SECOND CHORISTER: Here is the other, with which he held the
   reins.

THIRD CHORISTER: A part of his hip, or an upper leg—the left
   one.

FIRST CHORISTER: And here is the right. It fits with the other
   pieces.
   But how much is missing!

SECOND CHORISTER: How much is still unwept
                              for.   1260
   The unfound parts must grieve us all the more.

THESEUS: (*Howls*) No, I must keep control—of my hands and
     tears,
and perform in as decent a way as I can the rites
a father owes even these ugly hunks
of flesh and gore. My son, but now mere meat.
(*He picks up a part and looks at it*)
What was this? I haven't the vaguest notion,
but I set it down in sorrow, in reverence, in place
or not. Who knows? There was a handsome face,
a fine boy, a beautiful, noble boy.
Look how the gods answer a father's prayer!   1270
Cruel, vicious, and playful.
(*He places an ornament on the pieces*)
                         Take this gift,
as a token of my contrition.
(*To* SERVANTS)
                         Take him away,
and let the fire cleanse and restore those limbs.
Open the palace doors. Air the place out,
foul with scheming and blood. Let Athens resound
with loud lamentation.
                         Someone, go back to the field
and look for the tiniest specks that remain. Bring them
back here, to the flames.
(*He points to Phaedra's corpse*)
                         And as for her, a hole
dug somewhere in dirt that will hide her away
deep, where her deadly taint can no longer reach us.   1280

(*All freeze and the lights go to black*)

MEDEA

MEDEA

CHARACTERS

MEDEA, daughter of Aeëtes, king of Colchis, and wife of Jason
NURSE of Medea
CREON, king of Corinth who had received Medea and Jason as
   fugitives from Thessaly
JASON, usurping king of Thessaly, and former captain of the *Argo*
   on the quest for the Golden Fleece
MESSENGER
TWO SONS of Jason and Medea (mute parts)
CHORUS of Corinthians
SOLDIERS (mute parts)

SCENE: *Corinth, in the courtyard of Creon's palace.*

(MEDEA *is revealed, downstage. Upstage, her* NURSE *attends her.*)

MEDEA: O gods! Vengeance! Come to me now, I beg,
   and help me, you who protect the nuptial bed.
   Rise up, sharing my anger at this insult
   to me and you as well. Serious gods,
   watch over the lives of men and women, reward
   good and punish evil. Hecate, queen,
   I charge you, in whose name Jason once swore,
   punish that faithless man whose oath is broken,
   who is forsworn, and offers again his empty
   promises. Or else, in the absence of gods,   10

133

I pray to Chaos itself, to endless night,
to the dark lord and lady of death, and you,
the Furies, nightmare doyennes of writhing hair
and smoking torches, be present now and hear me.
You stood in awesome array at our wedding rite
and marriage bed. Attend him now again,
as he takes a new wife to bed. Shower on them
the catastrophe they deserve, an utter ruin
I hardly dare imagine. I call down curses
upon his head—not death, but worse than that.   20
Let him live. Through unknown cities, let him
wander, hungry, friendless, in fear for his life,
hated, homeless, and let him knock at the doors
of strangers, plead, and rudely be turned away.
    Let him, at such moments, remember me
and how it was when we were still married, and grieve
at his folly—madness to throw a life away.
Worst, I pray his children resemble him,
know the same incomprehensible grief,
while he reads in their glistening eyes the complaint   30
they need not pronounce in words. I have delivered
children, by whom I swear I shall be avenged.
    The Sun, who is mighty father of my race,
rises still in the east and sets in the west,
but he must pause, look down, amazed, appalled,
depart from his usual course, and bring to Corinth
death and destruction. No more will ships be required
to sail south and around the Peloponnese,
but will cross directly by roads that cover over
with salt water the land where Jason lived.   40
    I wish I believed but I don't. What retribution
there is, I shall have to contrive myself, devise
with my own two hands. My womanly hesitations
I must suppress, and civilization's restraints
in which I no longer believe. Did I ever? Do you?
Horror, we know, is real. The rest is a dream,
pretense, or a children's story we cannot
quite abandon. Heaven and earth recoil,

and we admit the truth of the cataclysm—
that, yes, this happens. This is the way things are.   50
Wounds, blood, the last death rattle of victims,
no one has trouble believing in them. I trust
in grief and rage. The labor of childbirth pales
compared to the bringing forth of the bloody truth
of what life is. Having been shamed already,
shameless I shall repay a wound with a wound.
His sin cries out for expiation—now!

(*They retreat to one side as* CHORUS *enters in procession*)

CHORUS: (*Celebrating the wedding of Jason and Creusa*)
    May the gods of the sky and sea attend
    and bless the marriage of Jason, our prince.
    Be kind to them, and grant they may have   60
    the full measure of happiness man
    and woman can find together. We pray,
    knowing the perils, knowing the odds,
    that they may look forward eagerly every
    time that the evening star appears
    with its sure promise of night's encounter.

FIRST CHORISTER: How lovely the bride, the envy of any
    Athenian maiden or Spartan girl.
    No Boeotian can match her in beauty.
    We, his subjects, may take some pride   70
        in his good fortune.

SECOND CHORISTER: To find a match for this matchless creature,
    one must raise one's eyes to the heavens,
    and think of the great gods' rare passions
        for special mortals.

FIRST CHORISTER: Only a hero like Jason could merit
    such a prize, or even aspire
    to joys one would think the gods might keep
        all to themselves.

SECOND CHORISTER: As in the constellations above,   80
  where one star will gleam, outshining the others,
  so her beauty and his deserving
      glitter and shine.

FIRST CHORISTER: As the bride surpasses all other brides,
  so does this husband surpass all other
  husbands. We wish them well as we take
      joy in their joy.

SECOND CHORISTER: See how his loving gaze on her cheek
  causes a gentle blush as the sun,
  when the shepherd beholds it at dawn, rouges   90
      the dewy meadow.

FIRST CHORISTER: New vows mark a new day,
  and what has gone before is ended.
  The place of the mad woman of Colchis
      is filled by the fairer

  Aeolian maiden. Let us rejoice,
  as he must rejoice, and sing the praises
  of her whom he takes in his arms and wish them
      joy and long life.

CHORUS: Come, Hymen, with burning torches,   100
  light the way along the dark hall,
  sing your suggestive songs, and rejoice.
  Raise the pinewood flambeaux higher,
  and sing as we drive away all shadows.
  Life and brightness grace the occasion
  in which each one of us shares the joy,
  raising our glasses to drink their health.

FIRST CHORISTER: (*Sees* MEDEA)
  There is one, of course, who steals away unhappy,
  who scuttles into the gloom, stopping her ears

against our songs and laughter that insult
and assault her spirit. I say let her begone.   110

SECOND CHORISTER: A foreign woman, let her go back to her own
  people, the land of her birth. Our ways were never
  her ways. She was never comfortable here.
  It's better for us, and better for her as well.

(CHORUS *takes seats at the sides.* MEDEA *returns to center stage.*)

MEDEA: (*To* NURSE) A nightmare—as if I were dead but forced to
    watch
  as the people I loved dearly and thought loved me
  don't mourn, but rejoice, dance at my wake. My corpse,
  off in a corner, hardly attracts their notice.
  I've nothing. Jason took all, my country, my father.
  Foolish, I followed him here, and now I'm abandoned,   120
  alone, a stranger among strangers. Or, worse,
  they all hate me. I deserved better than this,
  and those crimes I committed in love's name, for his sake,
  using my dark powers. But I'm set aside,
  tossed away as if I were nothing. . . . He cannot!
  My own brother, I killed for his sake, hacked
  in grisly bits and spread on the beach . . . and now,
  I wish he had a brother.
                          I have done evil,
  and may again! What love could accomplish, hate
  can also accomplish. The blood I've shed commands   130
  his fear if not his gratitude and respect.
  They say he had no choice, but that's never true.
  There's always death's way out. A sword point cuts
  through all the compulsions and threats. If he loved me,
  as I loved him, he would have refused, defied
  King Creon's whim, or fled for love and honor.
  Unloved, dishonored, I shall contrive such mischief
  as may remind the groom and bride and her father
  that sacred vows are not mere playthings, even
  of fatuous pompous kings. The torches blaze,   140

but my heart's flames will not be contained. His house
will be smashed, rubble, ashes, in which he shall lie,
sobbing among the ruins with even sharper
griefs than my own. I gave up a life for him!
I gave him the gift of his own life. He repays me
thus? His pledges broken, his words of love
all unsaid. It's Creon who did this, as if
Medea didn't exist. But I do. And the city
will know, for the world will mark its towering flames.

NURSE: Hush, I pray you. Keep your thoughts and threats   150
   to yourself. In shrewdness plot what you will, but patient
   and silent, biding your time, ready to strike
   when your victim is unwarned and unprepared.
   Bluster is nothing, but real hurt demands
   real hurt in return.

MEDEA: Trivial grief
   is easy to hide, but mine cries out for redress.

NURSE: Think what you need to do! It isn't shouting
   and empty threats you want but real revenge.

MEDEA: Fortune favors the bold; cowards are silent.

NURSE: So are the crafty—conspirators, spies, and assassins.   160

MEDEA: I'd rather be a mighty host advancing
   relentlessly . . .

NURSE: But you're only a woman, hopeless . . .

MEDEA: Nothing to hope is freedom, is nothing to fear.

NURSE: Colchis is far away. You've no resources.
   Your wealth is gone. What can you do alone?

MEDEA: Medea is still alive. In her you behold
rage, frenzy, fury, fire, and venom.

NURSE: I fear the king.

MEDEA: I don't. Our line is royal.

NURSE: They're armed men.

MEDEA: There are always dragon's teeth.

NURSE: You'll die!

MEDEA: Good.

NURSE: Flee!

MEDEA: Not any more.   170

NURSE: Medea!

MEDEA: I am Medea!

NURSE: You are a mother!

MEDEA: I know and am thinking of that at every moment.

NURSE: Then flee, for your children's sake and your own as well.

MEDEA: But first, revenge!

NURSE: They'll be after you.

MEDEA: Perhaps,
but I might devise something to slow them down.

NURSE: Your threats will undo you. Humble yourself. Remember
who you are, a woman and all alone.

MEDEA: The little that's left to me, no one can take—
    my spirit, my rage. But the king's gate swings open.
    His majesty, himself, in a grand appearance!   180

(*Trumpets sound.* NURSE *exits.* MEDEA *retreats to the side of the stage.* CREON *enters.*)

CREON: Medea? Still here? She is plotting mischief,
    I have no doubt. She wants revenge, will stop
    at nothing. These Orientals don't understand
    the value of human life the way we do.
    I wanted her killed, but, no, they wouldn't listen.
    My daughter and her new husband wanted her life
    spared, and I gave in. We settled on exile.
    But it wasn't wise or prudent. And I'm not happy.
    Let her begone at once and leave us in peace.
    (MEDEA *approaches* CREON)
    See how she comes forward, bold as brass!   190
    Keep her away. I don't want to see her or hear her.
    Let her obey a royal command. Exile
    doesn't allow her access at court.
    (*To* MEDEA)
                            Away!
    Keep your distance. You are an outlaw. Go!
    It's not permitted. This is disgraceful, awful . . .

MEDEA: But what have I done? Why have I been exiled?

CREON: It can't be a serious question.

MEDEA: I ask for justice.

CREON: I am a king. My word is law. That's it,
    right or wrong. Like it or not, obey.

MEDEA: Injustice cannot endure.

CREON: Complain to Colchis.   200

MEDEA: Let him take me back who brought me hither.

CREON: Don't be absurd! It's too late. He's remarried.

MEDEA: Divorced, exiled, but I was never heard.

CREON: Very well. I'm listening. Speak your piece.

MEDEA: Not with your ears only but with your heart,
listen. I know what pride can do. Decisions
that wavered once in the mind harden in air
as the words congeal to royal commands. I know,
for though I am now an object of pity, forsaken,
an exile, among strangers, I lived in a palace   210
and claim descent from a noble and godly line.
My father rules the steppes of Asia, the marshes
that flow into the Pontus, Scythian wilds,
and the crescent-shielded Amazons' home on the swift
Thermodon's banks. I drank from golden goblets
and listened to princes sue for my hand. Now I
bow my head and sue. Thus fortune toys
even with us who are royal. Power and glory
time can snatch away, and nothing remains
but memory to soothe or else torment,   220
according to what we remember, good or evil.
This only have I carried with me from Colchis,
the bitter wisdom—that one must learn to live
as if in the face of death, for each of us always
lives that way. Deeds, kindly or cruel,
are what we carry with us. I saved the *Argo*,
the flower of Greece, the heroes, demigods . . .
I did that. Of Jason and all the others,
his brave companions whose lives I held in my hands,
I am proud, and hold my head high even now,   230
bereft as I am, impoverished, outcast, and yet
the richest woman in Corinth. Castor and Pollux,
I saved, and Zetes and Calaïs. Lynceus, too.
Allies now, and kings, they owe their lives

to me. But disregard Jason. Him, I saved
only for myself. The others, I claim,
and for their sakes I appeal to you now for justice
or clemency, on the ground of the good service
I have done the state.
                              On the other side, my crime. . . .
But what crime am I said to have done, what law   240
broken? Shameful acts, I do confess
freely. But crimes? What charge is made against me?
Whom have I injured? Where are my evil gains?
If I'm to be punished, at least let me have my booty;
give me Jason, for whom I admit I have sinned.
    On my knees, I beg you, a suppliant, let me stay,
find some obscure retreat for me, some hovel,
modest, even mean, where I can live
outside the city walls. Show me some mercy
and do not drive me away, alone, into exile.   250

CREON: I'm not a violent man. I wield the scepter
    gently and with compassion—I do what I can
    for the poor and helpless everywhere. I try,
    and I think I'm known as a philanthropic man
    throughout the region. I've picked as a son-in-law
    an exile, after all. A fugitive, really—
    for King Acastus has a warrant out for Jason
    on account of what you two are said to have done
    to his father in Thessaly. But let that go. I'm sure
    if what Jason did were considered in isolation,   260
    he'd come out well enough. You were the one
    to beguile Peleas' daughters and teach—or mislead—
    so they cut their father into little pieces
    and boiled his body, and all to rejuvenate
    that weak old man! You are a ruthless woman,
    and dangerous. Jason, by himself, is benign,
    but you, alone . . . I hardly dare imagine
    what you might do, a woman in recklessness
    but a man in strength of will. I must purge my kingdom   270
    from the deadly poison I think you are. I'm sorry,

but there it is. For the sake of civil order
and my own peace of mind, you must go away.

MEDEA: You drive me hence? Then give me back my ship,
and its captain, too. Why should I flee alone?
We arrived together and share in our guilt: for him,
I killed King Pelcas, not for myself. We fled
together, killed my brother together. For him,
I deserted my father. You have it the wrong way round.
Taking my case on its own merits, I'm blameless.   280

CREON: You waste your words and, more to the point, my time.

MEDEA: Allow me one last request. My sons are guiltless.
Do not allow my taint to attach to them.

CREON: I shall be as a doting father to them, I promise.

MEDEA: I thank you, sir. And . . . I ask you one thing more.
By all that you hold holy, by this marriage day,
by the kindness of Fortune that blesses the city, I beg you,
stay my departure one more day. Allow me
a mother's farewell to her children, and one last kiss.

CREON: I don't trust you. You'll use the time for mischief.   290

MEDEA: What can I do in a day?

CREON: What can you not?

MEDEA: Would you deny me even a time for weeping?

CREON: I should. But I cannot. Very well, one day
to prepare for your exile and bid your sons farewell.

MEDEA: I am deeply grateful.

CREON: You are wasting time. One day!
   Then, if you're found on this side of the isthmus,
   you die. And no extensions and no appeals.
   You understand?
   (CREON *stares at* MEDEA *for a moment*)
             This interview is ended.
   You will excuse me now. I bid you adieu.
   I'm late as it is for my daughter's wedding feast.   300

(CREON *exits left;* MEDEA *exits right*)

CHORUS: How frail the little ships
   with which we venture forth
   on the huge sea!
   The winds are fickle. The shore
   dwindles away to nothing.
   We hide our fear,
   but only a fool would deny
   that doubt he must feel, rocking
   on dark waves,
   any of which could upset   310
   those fragile planks he assembled
   in tranquil weather.
   We long for the days gone by
   when no one ventured far
   from his own hearth.
   Nobody knew the craft
   the navigators use
   reading the heavens
   and nobody went to sea.
   We made do with our farms   320
   and what they yielded,
   and lived to a ripe old age.
   Now we have tastes for exotic
   treasures and spices.
   From distant shores come unruly
   passions and even crimes we
   could not have imagined.

There are monsters also, whose terror
comes only in part from their strangeness,
new pests and diseases,   330
but worst of all, by far,
is she, the lawless Medea,
wild as the ocean
that brought her into our haven,
relentless as any tornado
or waterspout,
but even more vindictive,
with harm that is hardly at random,
but fully intended.

FIRST CHORISTER: It seems to be an exaction   340
the gods are imposing upon us
for having undone
the clear commands of Nature.
Islands are separated
one from another
in accordance with some great purpose,
which we have contrived to frustrate,
and punishment follows.

SECOND CHORISTER: We admired the courage of Tiphys,
who piloted Jason's *Argo*,   350
but Tiphys is dead.
Is it coincidence merely?
Or is there a meaning, a message,
or even a warning?

FIRST CHORISTER: The ocean is hardly subtle
when winds howl and the water
pours over gunwales
of even the sturdiest vessels,
and sailors, clinging to wreckage,
swear solemn oaths   360
never again to set foot on
the deck of a ship, or to venture

across a cove.
But assume the sailor is rescued.
He forgets his fear and his promise.
A new day dawns,
with the sea looking smooth and tranquil,
its blue shot with the sunlight,
and beckons again.

SECOND CHORISTER: Harbors are busy, and cargo   370
   from the Indian Ocean piles up
   next to that of the Rhine.
   We learn to enjoy these trifles
   and tell one another it's progress,
   but think of the cost.
   The woman we welcomed among us
   is bearer of terrors more ghastly
   than those sailors live through.
   Resentment is boiling, and vengeance
   sighs as each breaker recedes on   380
   the darkening shingle.
   Its menace is hard to ignore, as
   is hers. She intends to do ill to
   our lives here in Corinth.

FIRST CHORISTER: It is said that the figurehead
   of the *Argo* was carved from the wood
   of Dodona's trees,
   oaks that were able to speak,
   and the figurehead retained   390
   its godly magic.
   They say it could warn the crew
   of the dangers that lay ahead.
   Why was it silent
   when the ship made fast in our harbor
   and she disembarked with her baggage
   of hurt and revenge?

SECOND CHORISTER: In its bed, the deep sea tosses,
   as if, in its sleep, it were dreaming
   terrible nightmares   400
   and trying to wake, to escape from
   grotesque unendurable horrors.
   We are awake and have no
   such hope of relief: we are forced to
   witness the ending.

(MEDEA *enters, hurrying out of the house. She is pursued by* NURSE.)

NURSE: Wait, child! Restrain your passion. Think!
   Get hold of yourself. For pity's sake! Listen!
   Listen to me, I beg you . . .
   (MEDEA *continues to wander about the stage, not paying*
     attention)
                        Mad as a Maenad,
   and just as frenzied, as if the god were coming
   to take possession. She is possessed. Her cheeks   410
   burn, and her eyes blaze with a holy fire
   I've never seen before and am terrified now
   to behold in the poor woman. She pants, she sobs,
   she screams, and then falls silent and picks at the hem
   of her garment. And then the fury begins again
   and stronger. I fear it will end in something dreadful.
   (MEDEA *approaches* NURSE *and stops, glaring*)
   I hope I'm wrong, but fear she's totally mad.

MEDEA: (*Aside*) There are no limits to love, nor should there be
   to hatred, for they are two aspects of the same
   passion. Life matters, or else it does not.   420
   If it does, then one must fight, risk everything,
   even disturb the balance and order we see
   in the cold heavens. And if not, then we risk
   nothing. The bear will continue to spin on its tail,
   and the waters of rivers will still pour into the sea,
   on and on, in a meaningless repetition.
   We look to these things for pattern, for purpose, believe

that our lives too must have some design, some plan. . . .
Who planned these things for me? What divine order
decreed that I should suffer so? I defy   430
the heavens themselves. Fierce as a wounded beast
I turn on my attacker to lunge and slash,
eager to bring him down to share my dying.
No fire can match the burning within my soul,
nor waterspout the gushing of hatred the gales
of my fury whip into spume. I shall devastate,
wreak such havoc as men and women shall speak of—
or whisper—in horrified awe for a thousand years.
      What was Jason thinking? Was it Creon he feared?
But what should a hero fear? How can a lover's   440
passion pale that way? A heart full of love
has no room left for cowardice. Compulsion
has nothing to say to love, can't speak a language
love would understand. But suppose he heard
Creon's threats and yielded? He still could have come
to speak to me, to explain, to bid farewell.
But not a word, as if he feared me, too.
The son-in-law of the king, he could have pleaded
in my behalf, for my children's sake, for mine,
that my banishment be postponed. But nothing, nothing.   450
I have but the single day I bargained for,
and that shall stretch out, for I shall make do,
will do such things in this one day that all other
days shall shrink, marvel, and mourn.

NURSE: Calm yourself.

MEDEA: The only calm for me is in death and ruin.
      As I go down, I shall also bring them down.

(*Exit* MEDEA)

NURSE: (*Calling after* MEDEA)
      What can you do, a woman alone? Your strength
      is nothing to theirs. You can only hurt yourself!

(*Enter* JASON)

JASON: How cruel a fate—hard in adversity, harder
   when it finds a cure for our ills. The medicine's bitter.   460
   Faithful to my wife, I die. Alive,
   for the children's sake, I must betray the mother.
   It's dreadful either way, but I choose the lesser
   evil, for the children, innocent, weak—
   but that's their strength, which is far greater than mine.
   One does those things one hates. But how to explain?
   What words will serve to beg her pardon?
(*Enter* MEDEA)

                                     Look
   at the terrible anguish. Passion. Fury. Love.

MEDEA: (*Surprisingly gently, at least at first*)
   We flee again, Jason. We flee—this time
   from each other. That other time it was for you, with you;   470
   this time it's you who are forcing me to leave
   our home. And where am I to go? To Colchis
   and the beach drenched with my brother's blood? What seas
   shall offer a safe haven? The Pontus? Hardly.
   Those places are closed, hostile to us, to me . . .
   I am exiled here but, tell me, where can I go?
   I go, I go. The son-in-law of the king
   commands, and I yield, can hardly refuse. I go
   uncomplaining. I agree, I deserve to be punished—
   for folly. For excess! The king is right to be angry.   480
   He ought to impose worse penalties—a dungeon,
   an oubliette, where I'd starve to death in darkness
   and heavy chains—for having been such a fool.
      Ungrateful man, remember the dragon's teeth
   and the armed men who sprang to life on the plain!
   Had it not been for me, you would have suffered
   a hideous ending then—but I bade you throw
   a stone in their midst, and they fell on each other and hacked
   each other to bits in a frenzied slaughter. Or think
   of my poor brother, dead, dismembered, scattered. . . .   490

Each gobbet of flesh a crime upon my head
for which I suffer now. Think of Peleas, too,
whom his daughters cut up. More butchery, and I
am guilty, guilty, guilty—I admit, insist.
And yet I ask, I beg, by the heads of our children;
by the monsters we conquered, the perils we survived;
by heaven and earth and sea; by Hecate, witness
to our wedding rites, I plead for mercy.
Happy and safe as you are, have pity on me,
who asks, as a suppliant asks, for a measure of peace. . . .   500
   Think what I gave away, was happy to give
for your sake—father, brother, native land,
my maidenhead, as well as the wealth of the Indies
and Scythian gold piled high . . . all of it gone,
spent, abandoned, squandered for you, for you.
This was the dower I brought. I ask for it back.

JASON: I tell you, Creon wanted you killed. I pleaded,
   begged for your life. By my tears he was moved
   to mercy, so that you are merely banished.

MEDEA: That is a punishment less severe? A blessing?   510

JASON: Go while you can. The anger of kings is dreadful.

MEDEA: The anger of kings? Or is it your new wife, Creusa,
   whose anger you fear? Is it for love you do this?

JASON: Love? Of her?

MEDEA: Or guilt!

JASON: Of what am I guilty?

MEDEA: Of what I have done, you, too, are guilty.

JASON: Why?

MEDEA: Whoever stands to profit from crime is guilty.
  My sins are therefore yours, for whose sake I sinned.
  Let all the world accuse me, then, but you
  must maintain that I am guiltless, as you are guiltless.
  Nobody dares to say what everyone thinks,   520
  but you know what they think.

JASON: That would be shameful.

MEDEA: And will you cling to a life you know to be shameful?

JASON: Medea, calm yourself. Think of our children.
  What I do is for their sake.

MEDEA: I disown them,
  reject, forswear, deny them. Shall Creusa inflict
  brothers and sisters on our children?

JASON: Yes.
  A queen to the sons of exiles, and foster mother
  to those who are helpless. Your quarrel is not with her.

MEDEA: Never! Mine is the line of Phoebus, but she
  is Sisyphus' infamous get, disgraced, dishonored!   530

JASON: Why do you want to ruin us both? I've done
  the best I could. And you should go now.

MEDEA: Creon
  has heard my modest prayer!

JASON: What do you want?
  Tell me what you would have of me.

MEDEA: (*Sarcastic*)   Of you?

JASON: I am hemmed in: on one side a king, on the other . . .

MEDEA: Medea! And I'm the worse by far. Let the king
and me contend with each other, with you as trophy.

JASON: I cannot bear it! Say what you want me to do,
I shall obey. But do not tempt the fates!

MEDEA: Till now, the fates have always been kind to me.   540

JASON: King Acastus is sworn to kill you.

MEDEA: Creon
is the nearer foe. Let us flee from them both,
for the one is a cousin, the other a father-in-law.
You may avoid the stain of kindred blood.

JASON: And if they unite, what can we do against both?

MEDEA: (*Laughing*) Those two, and Colchis, and Aeëtes also.
And the Scythians, too. The Pelasgians as well.
Together, we will destroy them all.

JASON: You jest.

MEDEA: You think so? But you would. You are not desperate,
as I am.

JASON: We have taken too long already.   550
You must go now.

MEDEA: Jupiter, hear me! Lord
of the thunderbolts, hear and stretch forth your hand with
      avenging
fire to shake the dull rock of the world.
In a pure, blind rage, strike, and let guilt
consume itself and destroy him, me, and all—
all of us together.

JASON: For this display
   of histrionics, there is no time left. Consider
   what you need for your flight. I shall supply
   whatever you want. You have only to ask.

MEDEA: I ask
   for my children. Give me my children. You can have new   560
   sons and daughters. I cannot. Let me have
   these as companions, comforters in my grief,
   and as protectors.

JASON: I wish I could do that,
   for your sake. But as a father, I have to think
   what's best for them. Creon would not permit it
   in any case, for, if they went with you,
   he would always fear them. Remember, I love them.
   Sooner would I part with life itself
   than with my sons.

MEDEA: (*Aside*)   Thus, he loves his sons?
   How good to know—for this is the tender place   570
   where I shall wound him, the perfect spot to strike.
   I'll beg him for this one, quite modest favor.
   (*To* JASON)
   Very well. But you'll let me say good-bye?
   Yes? A last embrace? A mother's kiss?
   You cannot deny me so little. Let my distracted
   words float away on the wind, like the smoke of fires
   that stings the eyes. My anger now is spent.

JASON: And is gone from my mind. Of course, you shall see the
      boys.
   I only ask that you keep control of yourself
   and try to stay calm for their sakes and your own.   580

(JASON *exits*)

MEDEA: Gone? Like that? He's forgotten who I am
  and what I've done! It's all fallen away,
  as if it had never happened. But I shall remind him.
  (*To herself*)
  Remember what you were and what you have done,
  how bloody your hands already, that cannot be further
  stained. There is a gift of shamelessness
  that few enjoy, but I am shameless, fearless,
  and, if I have to be, absolutely heartless.
  (*To* NURSE)
  Friend to my grief and misery, help me now!
  There is a robe, a treasure of our house,   590
  a gift of the Sun to his son, to King Aeëtes.
  There is also a necklace fashioned of gleaming gold
  and a gold tiara set with precious gems.
  Let my sons bring these precious objects
  as gifts for the bride. . . .
                              But let me first prepare them
  with exquisite poisons. Call on Hecate. Pray
  at awesome altars where smoky fires rise
  for the old magic, the powers of darkness and death.

(MEDEA *and* NURSE *exit*)

CHORUS: Nothing in nature, fire or gale,
  nothing in war, sharp sword edge   600
  or glittering spearpoint, terrifies
    as a woman's hatred.

  The raging torrents in springtime destroy
  houses, villages, tear down towns
  in blind fury, but hers is the greater
    and more destructive.

  The fire of passion burns in a hearth
  to sustain a household, but out of control
  it turns to conflagration and ruins
    the house and the city.   610

You cannot reason with Nature's rages.
You cannot argue with women, either,
when the fit is upon them. They seem to enjoy
   destroying themselves,

as if for the judgment of somebody watching,
spectators or jury, humans or gods,
as if the real blood that were spilled
   were merely stagecraft.

We pray that Jason may live in safety,
having already survived the perils   620
of raging ocean, of mortal battle.
   This danger is greater.

FIRST CHORISTER: It's better not to be one of the major
   dramatis personae. Our lives in the chorus
   are troubled enough. To witness this business
     is all we can bear.

SECOND CHORISTER: What is the point of those marvelous
   exploits?
You come back home to enjoy the glory
and wealth you have earned, but only find worse
   and more sordid troubles.   630

FIRST CHORISTER: Phaëthon dared what none of us would have,
   destroying himself and bringing ruin
across the Sahara. The risks of failure
   are truly dreadful,

but look at Jason. He succeeded,
and the lord of the ocean cannot forgive him.
Tiphys, the dead helmsman, is waiting
   to welcome his captain.

SECOND CHORISTER: Orpheus, venturing down to Pluto's
   dismal kingdom, contrived a return,   640
   but was he then happy? A frenzy of women
      tore him apart.

   A second time he crossed over the Styx,
   this time for good, and relieved to be where
   there may not be pleasure, but cannot be much
      occasion for fear.

FIRST CHORISTER: Some men venture for gold or glory,
   but others only reluctantly go
   to do the bidding of fate, to perform
      arduous tasks   650

   they cannot evade. Such was Jason,
   but not even this can excuse him from
   the ocean's resentment. The payment demanded
      is heavy indeed—

   for the waves fling up on the beaches glitter,
   polished stones that look to be gems,
   but then they take the treasure back.
      What little is left

   fades, turns dull, is revealed as worthless,
   as children who play in the surf soon learn.   660
   One might expect that the difficult lesson
      would last for a lifetime.

SECOND CHORISTER: The exploits of heroes are like that—
     splendid,
   but then, at the end, there's a dreadful reversal.
   Even a Hercules, striding the earth,
      is constrained and reduced

by the poisoned shirt, clinging, on fire.
What is the point of it? Virtue and strength,
honor and cleverness, come to the same
    deplorable ending   670

or even a worse than wickedness ever
is made to suffer. The soul cries out,
pities the pain, but feels more deeply
    the gross injustice.

And nobody learns, not even Idmon,
one who could read the future of others,
and perhaps even his own, but could not
    alter a thing.

He couldn't avoid the viper that waited
as if for thousands of years, fated   680
to hatch and bite the Argonaut, hunting
    on Libyan sands.

FIRST CHORISTER: What good is the gift then? How can we tell
    which are the blessings and which the curses?
    Better therefore not to be noticed.
        Keep your head down,

    live simply, a day at a time, and
    never adventure. The roads have dangers,
    the woods are worse, and the sea is the worst,
        cruel and vindictive.   690

(CHORUS turns to look as NURSE enters)

NURSE: My soul shakes at the terrible trouble brewing
    in her heart's cauldron. The fire crackles, the broth
    bubbles and seethes. Sun and moon grow pale
    at the monstrous thing she prepares. At her private shrine
    she recites her spells and performs the ghastly rites
    to marshal her old powers and summon the strength

from darknesses of the world to do such things
as I dare not imagine. The burning sands of the desert
and the frozen wastes of the far north come together
to conspire against mankind and the moderation   700
we take for granted. Serpents writhe into the light,
knotting with other serpents to form a swollen
and poisonous coil she shrieks with delight to behold.
Whatever is vile is lovely; whatever is darkest
causes her eyes to glitter. She prays to Horror
to accept her worship, bless her, inspire. Smoke
and sulphur rise up from the ground: she breathes them in
as if they were purest mountain breezes in Spring,
and her exhalations are dreadful. Curses and coughs
punctuate one another, and yet she thrives,   710
blossoms, looks much younger, and shines with a beauty
that terrifies more than it pleases.
                                        I watched those serpents
call out to their brothers and sisters—adders,
constrictors, and vipers—and lizards and newts assembled
in cold-blooded congregation. Meanwhile, from her chest
she produced the herbs of Eryx, the Caucasus' plants
spattered with gore from Prometheus' agony, poisons
the Arabs dip their arrows into, the juice
of forbidden roots the Sueban women gather
at night in their secret groves. The deadliest flowers   720
that bloom only at night, and the sickening galls
of dying trees she mixed together, the rarest,
most dangerous mosses, terrible molds, and powders
she'd made from the dried saps of noxious vines
cut from their roots with a bloodied sickle. . . .
                                        All these
she stirred together and boiled, chanting and moaning
as if in pain or ecstasy. These rites
I have seen in part before, but never these new
and hideous variations. She milks the serpents'
venom for poisons to add to the stew. And birds,   730
unclean carrion birds, she submerges alive.
The heart of a screech owl, still beating, she flings

into her loathsome pot. God knows what else. . . .
    You don't believe in these things? Civilized, Greeks,
you dismiss these primitive practices, superstitions
from far away. . . . It can't happen here, you say?
It's not that simple. The question she faces is whether
it feels worse to be evil in a good
and orderly universe, or admit the darker
and likelier choice—that there is no order. That chaos   740
whirls our meaningless lives this way and that way,
to make a pattern perhaps, as the soot that swirls
from the fire makes a smudge on the ceiling, but meaning
nothing at all, nothing, teasing, but nothing.
It is to that void she appeals, giving up what you,
and you, and you rely on.
                            Plants that are clipped
by the fingernails of a killer may have a power.
The way she disposes the nasty objects, the songs
she croons, may have an effect, or her rage alone
may be enough—the reckless rage of despair.   750
To hear her words is to feel the marrow chill,
and the muscles of the legs go slack in a dizzy
feeling of disconnection with the earth.
Agony has its own laws. Ice can burn,
as horses dying of thirst can try to drink fire.
To such extremes is she driven, and from her wrongs
only worse and larger evils can come.
    But I hear her crooning. Listen, if you can bear it.

(*Enter* MEDEA)

MEDEA: I invoke the dead, demand they rouse themselves
    from their grand indifference. Gods of the underworld,   760
    and you, the suffering ghosts of Tartarus, hear me
    as I call from my abyss to yours. Rise up
    and come to my aid. Let Tantalus drink
    a toast to the bride and groom! Let Ixion's wheel
    cease to spin, and let him stand on the firm
    ground to bless the nuptial rites. Let the endless

toil of the Danaids be interrupted, their leaky
urns put aside for the time. I need your hands
to help me now. I call for a general pardon—
except for Sisyphus, father to King Creon.   770
Let his stone weigh heavier, let his slope
be steeper, slippery, sliding the boulder backward.
    But the rest I summon, and call on Hecate first,
the moon goddess, ghastly queen of the night.
Be with me now, in your most dreadful aspect.

        For you I unbind my hair,
        for you I take off my shoes,
        and walk in a circle barefoot,
        as we did in the secret groves,   780
        around the sacred trees,
        calling on heaven to open
        and bring us rain.

        The round of the sun and moon,
        the round of the sea and land,
        of seasons of earth and heaven,
        of men's lives and of cities',
        around the sacred trees,
        call on heaven to open
        and bring us relief.   790

(*She offers gifts to Hecate*)

        Hecate, hear me! I offer
        these wreaths that bloodied hands
        have fashioned of serpent coils
        that Typhoeus wore when he struggled
        against mighty Jupiter's throne.

        I offer the blood of Nessus,
        and feathers the Harpy left
        when she fled from the Argonaut Zetes.
        Their power is your power,

their honor is yours, and the passion.   800
Accept my gifts, O queen!

Come to us now, with terror,
shedding your ghastly light
that makes strange the familiar
and shows us the other side,
which is also a part of the truth.

At the moon's eclipse, we have beaten
the bronze gongs to restore you
to your rightful place in the heavens.
To you, on the bloody altars   810
we have made our sacrifice, bowing
heads, with our hair in the ashes,
and chanting the magical words,
waving the yew and the cypress
that grow by the Stygian river.

I offer blood for blood,
cutting myself like a Maenad,
letting the drops flow forth.
The hand that holds the dagger
is yours, as the arm that receives   820
the wound is yours also.
Accept the gift of my life
and lend me your dismal powers.

(*She cuts her arm and lets the blood flow upon the altar. She
waits for a moment, looks up, and then speaks as if to a friend.*)

Yes, my lady, I know. I have come to you often before. Too often,
I'm afraid. And you have always been kind to me. And I am
grateful. And I have been stupid. It's Jason again, still, always. But
you have helped me before, and I swear this is the last time.
Indulge me and grant my prayer.

(She takes a phial and pours its contents onto the robe she has set out)

Poison Creusa's garment,
and let the flames consume her,
burning her flesh and her marrow,   830
and making her vile blood boil.

Within this gold is fire
Prometheus gave me—its pain
is what he feels as the bird
slashes and pecks at his liver.
Mulciber's sulphurous fire,
and Phaëthon's fire I add,
to flames the great Chimaera
vomited forth, and Medusa's
terrible gall. Give sting   840
to these pretty poisons, my lady;
let them deceive the eye
and even at first the touch.
But then, and then, and then,
let them begin their magic,
penetrating the skin and
veins and the bones with their burning.
Let smoke arise from her body
as if, on a spit, she were roasting
alive, her hair incandescent,   850
and let her howls float on the air like
the world's loveliest music.

(She repeats the dance step of the opening of her prayer)

The round of the sun and moon,
the round of the sea and land,
of seasons of earth and heaven,
of men's lives and of cities',
around the sacred trees,

call on heaven to open
and bring us relief.

(*The fire on the altar blazes up. A bell rings three times.*)

My prayers are heard. The fire has blazed, and the bell   860
rings true. Now are my powers summoned.
Let my sons be brought that they may take these
gifts of mine to the bride.
(*The* TWO SONS *are brought in*)
                              Go, my children,
born to a most unfortunate mother. These
nice gifts may help you to win the love
of your new stepmother. Take these presents to Creusa,
and then return for a last embrace from your mother.

(*The* TWO SONS *exit toward the palace.* MEDEA *exits the other way.*)

FIRST CHORISTER: What was that all about?
    Some odd and primitive rite,
    but nothing for us to fear   870
    who don't share her superstitions.

SECOND CHORISTER: Still, she is not unimpressive.
    Emotion like that is alarming.
    Her cheeks flush and then pale,
    she tosses her hair in anger,
    and sets her jaw in a fury
    that even threatens our king.
    One would hardly think an exile,
    a single, powerless woman,
    could even pretend to such menace.   880

FIRST CHORISTER: She ought to control her emotions,
    but she paces, mutters, and mumbles,
    as if she were crazy, as if she
    weren't a human, but rather
    a tigress whose cubs have been taken.

It's not superstition to fear her,
but prudent. Who knows what she's thinking
or what she feels driven to do?
I wish that this day were ended,
and fear what the daylight remaining   890
may offer our unwilling witness.
We're relieved at each moment that passes,
but dread those before us—each one
tremulous with a disaster
we can feel in the air and our bones.

(*Enter* MESSENGER, *running, from the direction of the palace*)

MESSENGER: Disaster! Catastrophe! Ruin! Complete devastation!
   The props of the kingdom are fallen, our city is toppled,
   and father and daughter are dead. They are nothing but ashes.

FIRST CHORISTER: Tell what has happened.

MESSENGER: A trick.

FIRST CHORISTER: Explain
   yourself.

MESSENGER: The trick that can take a king: treacherous gifts.   900

SECOND CHORISTER: Treacherous, how? You aren't telling us
   much!

MESSENGER: What is there to tell of such absolute ruin?
   The fire rages, the house is fallen, the city
   burns and quakes with terror.

FIRST CHORISTER: Let water be brought!

MESSENGER: But that is the trouble! Water feeds these flames,
   and they only burn the brighter. Nature's undone . . .

(*Enter* MEDEA *and* NURSE, *in time to hear this last speech*)

NURSE: (*To* MEDEA) My lady, flee. At once. You can still get away.
　　Go at once, wherever you will, but go!

MEDEA: Me? Go? But surely not! Had I gone
　　before this, I would come back to look and listen.   910
　　To savor every instant.
　　　　　　　　　　　　But it's not done.
　　Started only. There's more, and better and better.
　　I feel merely the skin's initial tingle
　　of those first steps of a long journey. My stride
　　is not yet reached. There is much to dare and endure.
　　The vengeance is only started. That love I felt
　　for Jason is not yet spent. It has turned to hatred
　　and seethes like lava. I must be stronger than rock.
　　Honor is gone, and all proportion. Nothing
　　can touch my pure purpose, or tame my spirit.   920
　　The strength I have summoned is great, and my only duty
　　now is to use it, to wring the last cry of pain
　　from that man's throat! What I have done thus far,
　　was nothing, a preface, a light-hearted overture.
　　The serious business that follows will make my famous
　　dark deeds seem parlor tricks for children,
　　or a girl's pranks. Now, I am an angry woman,
　　I am Medea. My apprentice term completed,
　　I shall address myself to a masterwork.
　　Anyone can cut a brother's head off—   930
　　that happens every day. And people steal
　　their father's treasure and run away—that's common,
　　hardly enough to arouse particular comment
　　at the village well. To arrange that an old man's daughters
　　should inflict on their father a horrible death shows promise,
　　but in relative terms is nothing, for I shall do now
　　such dreadful, such astonishing things. . . .
　　　　　　　　　　　　　　　　The children
　　are the way to reach him. Had he and Creusa offspring,
　　anyone could make a respectable plan.

What I must do is acknowledge the bitter truth   940
of what he did, taking my two sons from me
and claiming them as his own, their own. No longer
my children? Very well! It's hard,
but they shall pay for their father's crimes—as happens
often in this vile world.

                            My brain's cold logic
chills my heart. My limbs flutter. The rage
gives way, and a mother's concern returns, unbidden,
and altogether wrong. You heard him say it!
He would keep them for himself. They are not mine!
Their blood is not my blood. I will abide   950
by my lord's decree, and we'll see if he can stand it.
They'll be better off—who would endure with a father
like that, with a mother like this? Better be rid
of such an unspeakable past and future. They'll die,
innocent.

                    That happens, too, in the world.
My brother was innocent, too. Much good did that do him.
My tears are a nonsense, not for him, or for them,
but only myself. An indulgence. They will not deter
or delay me for more than the instant it takes to wipe
my face with a fist already clenched.

                                        Love them?   960
I have. I do. And will, after they're dead.
Much good will that do them or me. It's hard,
but either way, I lose them. I have lost
all, have nowhere to turn, must strike back, piling
griefs upon griefs as exaction for mine.

                                    Love them?
They would have been my solace, their hands soothing
my troubled brow, their kisses healing my wounds.
He took them from me; now I will take them, tear them
from him, and his tears will gush hotter than mine.
Children, come here!

                        I wept Niobe's tears   970
for sons. . . . Not seven but two, only the two.
But now they shall have at last a younger brother,

as I tear from my womb a monstrous vengeance, kin
of my dead father and dead brother. Our blood
shows itself in awful profusion.
                                The Furies
assemble, waving their torches: the garish light
stains all the world with blood. A hellish host
dances, cavorts, while serpents writhe and coil,
lashing their tails. Whom does Megaera seek?
These children? Jason? Me? Does it matter? My brother,   980
my poor brother, Absyrtus, calls out for justice,
with each of his scattered limbs, as if they had mouths,
a whole chorus, complaining.
                                And they shall be paid,
abundantly. Thrust the burning brands here,
here to my breast. Tear, burn, and hurt
however they will. There's nothing I cannot endure.
(*The* TWO SONS *enter*)
Yes, my children, come here!
(*To the* ELDER SON)
                                You will go to your uncle,
who asks for you, a solution to all our problems.
(*Kills him*)
Accept this victim, ghost, and be appeased.
(*Noises off*)
What is that sound? Armed men coming to kill me?   990
It won't be so easy.
(*To the* YOUNGER SON)
                                Come, we'll go to the roof.
Don't be afraid. We'll stay together.
(*To the corpse*)
                                And you,
you'll come with us, too.
(*To herself*)
                                O my soul, be strong!
This isn't some piece of secret business, but grand
and public, and I must do it with proper flair.

(*Exit* MEDEA, *carrying the corpse of one son and leading the other.*
JASON *enters, armed, and leading* SOLDIERS. *He addresses the
citizens.*)

JASON: Citizens, hear me! You who are faithful and mourn
    the sad fate of your prince! Lead me to her!
    Show me where she is, the butcher, the witch,
    and I shall make her answer for this and pay
    for what she has done. She is inside the house? Then
      burn it,   1000
    with her inside. Raze it, down to the ground.

MEDEA: (*Appearing on the roof*)
    A queen again, mistress of all that I see. . . .
    Everything's back, restored to me now. My father,
    my poor brother, Colchis, the Golden Fleece.
    I am a virgin again, newborn, unsullied.
    This is the first moment of my new life.
    The deed is done, but the vengeance only begins,
    and cool, cool. . . . For my anger is gone. I'm sad,
    deeply sorry for what I have done. But it's done,
    and nothing can change it now. I have reached a truth,   1010
    a terrible and incontrovertible truth,
    from which—I confess—I take a kind of joy.
    (*She looks down and sees* JASON)
    There he is, the necessary man—
    for nothing I have done has any meaning
    unless he sees it, feels it, and cries out.

JASON: Up there! She's there. Somebody, bring torches.
    We'll set the roof ablaze. She'll jump or burn.
    But either way . . .

MEDEA: No, Jason. No.
    I'm not the point. It's a funeral pyre, yes,
    but for your sons. Poor Jason! Your wife is dead,   1020
    and your father-in-law, too? A horrible death

I arranged for them. This son of yours also
is dead. See? And this is about to die.

JASON: No! By the gods, you cannot! I beg you, don't.
In the name of all we've been through together. . . . Guilt
is mine, and I should die. But spare the boy.

MEDEA: The guilt is yours, yes. And I will strike you
where you will feel it. . . . Here!
(*She indicates the living* SON)
                                        The sword goes here.
To see if a man who abandons wife and mother
is capable of feelings.

JASON: The one is enough.   1030

MEDEA: One? You don't understand. I reject such business
as measure, limit, proportion, counting. Two
is not enough. A thousand would not be enough.
If, in my ovaries, children of yours were lurking,
I'd stab each one to death with a pin.

JASON: You're mad.
You're altogether mad, utterly crazy!
But I won't plead any more. Do what you will . . .
but get it over with.

MEDEA: I'll take my time.
Creon gave me a whole day! What's the hurry?

JASON: Have pity, Medea! Kill me instead.

MEDEA: Die!   1040
(*She slays the second* SON)
It's done! You see? You see? You recognize
the wife you loved, ungrateful man? Remember
who I was and who I am. I go now.

(*She gestures with her arms. A huge chariot drawn by two*
   dragons descends from the sky.)
The air is my highway. Dragons will carry me off.
Your sons, I leave to you as I ascend
into the air, on my wonderful wingèd car.

(*She throws down the bodies of the two dead sons. She gets into the*
chariot and is borne away.)

JASON: What in the name of hell. . . ? A wingèd car?
   But there are no gods. No gods! There are no gods.

AGAMEMNON

AGAMEMNON

CHARACTERS

THYESTES' GHOST, uncle of Agamemnon, he has returned to earth
for vengeance against the house of his brother, Atreus
CLYTEMNESTRA, wife of Agamemnon, who has been plotting with
Aegisthus against her husband
NURSE of Clytemnestra
AEGISTHUS, son of Thyestes by his incestuous union with his
daughter, and lover of Clytemnestra
AGAMEMNON, son of Atreus, king of Argos, and leader of the
Greeks at Troy
EURYBATES, herald of Agamemnon
CASSANDRA, daughter of Priam, captive of Agamemnon
ELECTRA, daughter of Agamemnon and Clytemnestra
STROPHIUS, king of Phocis
ORESTES, son of Agamemnon and Clytemnestra (mute part)
CHORUS of Argive women
CHORUS of captive Trojan women
PYLADES, son of Strophius (mute part)
ATTENDANTS of Agamemnon (mute parts)

SCENE: *Mycenae, in the courtyard of Agamemnon's palace.*

(AEGISTHUS *is revealed, downstage, deep in thought. Upstage,* THY-
ESTES' GHOST *appears.*)

173

THYESTES' GHOST: From the dank murk of Tartarus' pit, Thyestes
  appears, so full of hate he cannot say
  which realm he despises more: the dreadful place
  I flee, or the kingdom of light where those I meet
  quake, quail, fall dumb, or else cry out
  in satisfactory horror. My father's house
  I see before me or, more to the point, my brother's
  cursèd house. This is the seat of Pelops'
  ancient awful line. In that throne room,
  they sit, proud lords, wield the scepter of power,   10
  and in that room they hold their feasts. Disgust
  clutches my vitals still and makes me long
  for the fetid pools of the Styx that monsters guard,
  where monstrous torments punish odious sinners
  extravagantly and yet never enough.
  There, Ixion whirls on his dizzying wheel,
  and Sisyphus toils with his rock up endless hills.
  There, Tityus writhes while the vulture tears
  at his living liver, and Tantalus reaches up
  to the teasing branch, or down to the mocking water   20
  that babbles a strict diet of taunt and insult
  on which he feasts and drinks his filthy fill.
  Yet are their crimes trifles compared with mine,
  as mine are peccadilloes to my brother's
  wreck of civilization's basic assumptions.
  If Tantalus hungers and thirsts, my stomach writhes
  in philosophical nausea: my three children,
  my own flesh, have I eaten. Their blood have I drunk.
    But then, to perfect my guilt and taint, my flesh,
  now used to sinning, sought itself otherwise,   30
  in forbidden embrace with my own daughter, my child,
  who bore me a child, her son and also brother,
  the young Aegisthus, my son and also grandson—
  and only hope—or so the oracle said:
  thus and thus must I do, to contrive revenge
  that revenge I lived for, reckless, sinned and died for,
  bloody and total, confounding nature, dismaying
  the gods themselves: to Atreus and his house,

horrors to make my home in the underworld
quake in fear and a kind of admiration.   40
And now, I see at last, as a farmer does,
the yield of all that work. The stinking manure
I've spread on the fields of human pretension has brought
that sweet and dainty harvest of retribution
of which I've dreamt. Agamemnon, king of kings,
and lord of lords, whose glorious flapping banner
Argive heroes saluted, he whose word
darkened the seas with a thousand ships, comes home,
the victor, to be brought low, to feel the pain
of mortal blows, not struck on the field of honor,   50
but in his very chamber—by the wife
of his bed and bosom, crazy with grief and rage
and guilt! It is now at hand: the blood and the sharp
edge of hammered metal of the sword
call out to one another as lovers might.

    Aegisthus, rouse yourself. Your father is come
to cheer you on in your dread purpose—for this
one deed I begat you, this one moment
I did a terrible thing to my poor daughter.
Think of her! Think, even, of me   60
and rouse yourself to dare the terrible thing!
(AEGISTHUS *gets up and hurries off stage*)
    Now that my son is up and about, the sun
may rise to show the horrors of the day
clearly while I return to the land of night.

(THYESTES' GHOST fades. CHORUS *of Argive women enters.*)

FIRST CHORISTER: Fortune is an impish god.
    The wealth and power she can give
    is often a trick or joke—the smug
    fall abruptly from their thrones,
    and she is amused to see it. Marble
    of palace floors can heave like the sea,   70
    tossing about the proud and mighty
    as if they were toys of an angry infant.

SECOND CHORISTER: Settled cities with theaters and temples
   suddenly turn to trackless jungles,
   Libyan quicksands, or arctic glaciers.
   Kings who were feared and learned to enjoy it
   acquire themselves the sweat of the terror
   of helplessness: no step is safe.

FIRST CHORISTER: What have the walls of the palace watched
   but crime that answers to terrible crime?   80
   What laws do they obey, what shame
   do they feel, what sacred bonds do they
   respect in those impressive chambers?
   In there, Bellona rules, her scepter
   dripping with blood to look like a torch,
   and Erinys, too proud to allow
   pride in mortals she brings down.

SECOND CHORISTER: War and treachery work their mischief,
   but, even without them, kingdoms give way
   under their own weight as the line   90
   weakens. A fatal taste for comfort
   undermines the courage and will.
   In another, lesser house, the change
   might pass unnoticed for generations;
   prominence and power invite
   a terrible testing of any flaw.
   The tall tree, the winds blow down;
   the high hill, the lightning strikes.

CHORUS: Whomever Fortune raises up,
   it is only to dash down into pieces.   100
   Better to live a modest life,
   obscure enough to escape the envy
   of men and the gods' terrible notice.
   In a frail boat, we hug the shore,
   dreading the wide expanse of water
   braver and greedier sailors dare:
   safe at home, we hear of their wrecks.

(CHORUS *arranges itself as part of the audience.* CLYTEMNESTRA
enters, accompanied by her NURSE, *whom she addresses.*)

CLYTEMNESTRA: Utterly lost, with nothing left to hope for,
    no way of going back . . . I was a wife,
    honest and chaste. No more, and what's undone   110
    cannot be mended. The river runs one way:
    downward, with no returning, and regrets
    are useless now. The only path to take
    is deeper into crime, where the faint heart
    fears to go. What other way remains?
    There have been faithless wives before, ablaze
    with passion, hatred, or merely guilt's own torments,
    and they have dared the great and dreadful deeds
    of woman's compass. Think of Medea's passion
    and what it drove her to! I must take courage,   120
    which is desperation's twin. We could run away,
    my lover and I, but that was the way of my sister,
    simpering Helen. I must meet that challenge
    with something better, braver, and true to myself.

NURSE: These fits of yours of anguished brooding scare me.
    What rashness do you contemplate, O queen?
    Illustrious daughter of Leda, your great soul
    knows no limits—that alarms me, too.
    Forbearance is not your gift, but there are times
    when reason fails and one must fall back to patience.   130

CLYTEMNESTRA: Passion and patience are always strangers. My
      fears,
    hatreds, jealousies, lust, and my shame, too,
    are seething together. I feel my soul on fire,
    maintaining a lively boil. Or say I am tossed
    back and forth among the capricious winds
    of the spirit's storms. In such foul weather, sailors
    prefer to remain ashore, but there's no harbor,
    no protection, and, if there were, the tiller
    is broken, the vessel careens, and in my torment

I dream of release and even begin to long   140
for that disaster by which it will come.
When reason is gone, and hope, what good is patience?
I watch, as from a great height, my undoing
and give my fate into the care of chance.

NURSE: Knowing that chance is blind? It makes no sense!

CLYTEMNESTRA: Sense itself can turn to utter nonsense.

NURSE: If there's nothing to do, then do—and say—nothing!

CLYTEMNESTRA: In palaces, there are never any secrets.

NURSE: Repenting of your old crimes, you plan new.

CLYTEMNESTRA: There's no going back; there's nothing left to
     lose.   150

NURSE: As sins worsen, their punishments will worsen.

CLYTEMNESTRA: For some disease, the knife is the only cure.

NURSE: But save extremest remedies for last!

CLYTEMNESTRA: Who supposes himself to have a choice?

NURSE: Think of those holy marriage vows you took.

CLYTEMNESTRA: For ten years have I thought, in rage and
     sadness.

NURSE: Consider that he is the father of your children!

CLYTEMNESTRA: I remember he was the father to Iphigenia,
     to whom he showed a scanty tenderness.

NURSE: The fleet was becalmed. He did, in terrible sorrow,   160
    only what the cruel god demanded.

CLYTEMNESTRA: The god? But I, myself, am descended from
      gods!
  I cannot blot from my mind the hideous picture
  of a young girl in a wedding dress! The altar
  was decked with flowers, fit for a wedding day,
  and Calchas, the priest, shuddered, as he pronounced
  the detestable oracle. On Pelops' house
  there is a curse that blood cannot wash out,
  for fresh blood is spilled, demanding more.
  Crime is heaped upon crime, and the innocent girl   170
  dies for a deal with the winds to enable war
  and murder: her freshet of blood becomes a river
  that's wider and deeper all the time. In Troy,
  they fought as much among themselves as with Trojans,
  in a sordid squabble for spoils. Chryseïs, the priest's
  daughter, he took, and then Cassandra, the god's
  own girl, blessed or cursed. These scandalous stories
  Greeks tell of themselves, as if in pride!
  Calchas could dictate Iphigenia's death,
  but not the return of Chryseïs to her father.   180
  Agamemnon cannot claim to be helpless,
  obedient to the dictates of the gods.
  For ten years, he entertained himself
  with one barbaric mistress after another—
  whoever was pleasing, even Achilles' Briseïs.
  The plague, the schism in camp, the war itself
  were nothing but lust, and petulance, and pride,
  with intervals now and again of actual fighting.
  Now that it's over and done with, he comes home
  with Cassandra in his train, so smitten with love   190
  he is unashamed of being a captive's mate
  and, after that bloodshed, son-in-law to Priam.
    I must be bold and strike before I am stricken.
  To hesitate a moment, allow a qualm,
  is to welcome ruin. For my own children's sake

I steel myself—to keep them from the care
of a stepmother the whole world knows is crazy.
My own life, I reckon as worthless. My blood
runs through my body for but one reason now—
to shed his. Of what should I be afraid?   200
I pray only to see, before I die,
or even as I die, Agamemnon, dead.

NURSE: O my queen, consider, I beg you! Think
how Agamemnon comes in glory and triumph,
Europe's hero, conqueror of Asia,
arriving home with booty and his train
of captives. And you dare to challenge him
whom mighty Achilles could not outface, nor Ajax,
not even Hector, bulwark against the Greeks,
or Paris, skillful archer that he was.   210
How can a woman's guile presume to compare
with the courage and strength of such heroes as these?
Will you attempt what the Amazon queen herself
could not accomplish, battle-ax in hand,
and a savage shield in the other glinting bright
in the morning sun? The victor is come home
and can you think, if you raise your hand against him,
the Greeks will not avenge him? Comrades in arms,
they will not permit such insult to their honor.
Horses will tramp the earth into mud, and ships   220
will blacken the sea's wide expanses of blue.
They are bound to one another, and you defy
them all if you strike at one. Control yourself,
or rather let your mind control your passions,
and try, lady, to set your soul at peace.

(NURSE *exits.* CLYTEMNESTRA *watches but does not follow.* AEGIS-
THUS *enters and speaks to the audience.*)

AEGISTHUS: The hour has come my soul has always dreaded.
How can I fear the aim of my existence
from my first breath and before? If I fail now,
then I am useless, worse than worthless, vile.
Let my destruction result from my own effort,   230
glorious and desperate, rather than gods'
and my forebear's disgust. Already damned,
I must be reckless, not only brave but shameless. . . .
(*To* CLYTEMNESTRA)
Partner in evil and danger, Leda's noble
daughter, let us face it together. Your husband's
time has come. His debt must at last be paid
for that blood he owes you. Think of your daughter, think
of yourself and your heart's grief and rage. Be brave.

CLYTEMNESTRA: I revered him once. I can remember how,
when I was a girl, we loved each other. Time   240
passes and we change, but not altogether,
and memory betrays us. Whatever happened
to those sweet youngsters he and I used to be?

AEGISTHUS: Control yourself! You cannot afford these flights!
Do you suppose that Agamemnon remembers
your marriage vows? Never mind your own
transgressions, which are trivial. Think of his—
arrogant, public, proud, impossible flauntings
of bad faith and bad conduct. Only Troy
kept the Greeks from turning on him, a tyrant   250
who happened to be their leader. Do you believe,
now that Troy is reduced to ruin, he
will return from that epic blood bath, gentled, chastened,
modest, loving, and good? Proud when he left,
he will be prouder, grander now with the gold
and slaves and whores he and his comrades shared.
And will you share your bed with Cassandra? Or she
share her bed with you? The god's own darling,
she will leave you nowhere to stand, sit, or lie down.

CLYTEMNESTRA: Aegisthus, do you speak for me or yourself? 260
    A warrior has some leeway. A king can enjoy
    his victory. A wife puts up with this,
    as the wife's lover cannot afford to do,
    for where does that leave him? My guilty heart
    will not allow me to judge my husband's behavior
    more harshly than I judge my own. Let us
    forgive each other, for pity's sake and love's.

AEGISTHUS: Are kings, who are viceroys of great gods,
    to break rules they enforce for lesser men?
    A throne is no easy chair, but the seat of the law   270
    whose majesty a king must either maintain
    or else, for himself and everyone, defile.

CLYTEMNESTRA: He pardoned my sister, Helen. Joined again
    to Menelaus, she offers a hope of healing.

AEGISTHUS: Menelaus never took a mistress.
    His heart had not, in all those long years, strayed
    as Agamemnon's has. Had you been blameless,
    you should have been at peril nonetheless,
    for those whom a king hates, for whatever reason,
    are condemned unheard, for having caused him twinges   280
    of bad conscience—as if that were a crime.
    What will you do? Go home, disgraced, to Sparta?
    You know well enough you've no choice but to kill him.

CLYTEMNESTRA: But why? Our secret is safe! No one
        suspects . . .

AEGISTHUS: There are no secrets. Servants will always blab.

CLYTEMNESTRA: Only pay them enough and they'll hold their
        peace.

AEGISTHUS: Bought silence can always be outbid.

CLYTEMNESTRA: Why do you speak these cynical words? I
    remember
what it used to feel like to be a lady,
a queen, an honest wife. . . . How can I trade   290
that life I had for one with an outcast like you?

AEGISTHUS: Instead of a son of Atreus, you shall have
a son of Thyestes . . .

CLYTEMNESTRA: Yes, and grandson also.

AEGISTHUS: It was what Apollo commanded. I'm not ashamed.

CLYTEMNESTRA: You should be. You cannot put blame on the god
who hid his face from what your father did.
They say the world went dark. And in his hate,
your father bred you up in spite, to foul
a marriage bed, which is what we do each time.
I hate the sight of you. Go! Leave me alone.   300
A king returns to his city, home, and wife!

AEGISTHUS: I'll go if you want. I'm not afraid of exile.
I'll go. Or, if you wish it, I will fall
on my sword or plunge it into my body, and gladly.
Unless it be with you, I have no life.

(CLYTEMNESTRA *hesitates*)

CLYTEMNESTRA: (*Aside*) Would he? Could I bear it if he did?
(*To* AEGISTHUS)
We have sinned together. That's a kind of bond.
There is, in crime, a marriage, or antimarriage.
We're stuck with each other. Come, in this dark time,
there is much to be done. Let us make our plans.   310

(*They exit.* CHORUS *of Argive women rises and marches onstage.*)

CHORUS: Sing, sing the praise of Apollo;
        put on his garland,
   and sing of the god who grants on occasion
        the power of foresight.
Wave the fragrant branch of the laurel
        in the four directions,
   and worship the god whose terrible brightness
        so often is blinding.

FIRST CHORISTER: Who can riddle the long odds
        of the future's secrets?   320
The prophet Tiresias' daughter Manto
        was also a prophet,
sat on the three-legged stool at Delphi
        and said what would happen.
She was the one who gave the instruction—
        or was it a warning?—
to honor Apollo and offer him homage.
        We know he likes music,
but what can we guess of the tastes of a god
        who insists on the best?   330
Nothing bombastic or vulgar will do.
        My recommendation
is to try for what's simple and unassuming—
        in other words, honest—
as if we were praying, for gods can attend
        to a heart's performance,
which is, as artists hate to admit
        a frightening business.
Songs to the gods are like fights in arenas,
        life-or-death battles.   340

SECOND CHORISTER: We sing to Apollo, but must not neglect
        his Olympian comrades.
If there be gods, as poets have told us,
        they are listening in
at least on occasion—Jupiter, Juno,
        and all of the others—

delighting to hear their names in our paeans,
        or mildly diverted.
Let us, like courtiers, try to conceal our
        inhibiting stage fright. . . .   350
Unless we assume they take some enjoyment
        in knowing we sweat
as we sing of their power, try to placate them,
        beg them to pardon
our many transgressions, and thank them for favors
        we owe to their whims.
So Agamemnon, voyaging homeward,
        is framing his prayers
in which we must join him, hoping the gods
        will continue to smile,   360
sparing our leader and also his subjects.
        We are not crazy,
and after his exploits and arduous journey
        will welcome him warmly,
and join in prayers he offers with cattle:
        the unblemished victims
will bleed on the altar, as we shall give thanks that
        the blood is not ours.

FIRST CHORISTER: Hear us, Minerva, child of the thunder,
        who helped in the triumph   370
poets will celebrate, mentioning always
        the favor you showed us.
And you, Diana, goddess of crossroads,
        protect him who travels
and bring him back home in safety and peace,
        for his sake and ours.
We know how your anger can ruin the wicked
        or merely impious
and remember how Niobe, Tantalus' daughter,
        was turned to a statue   380
that nonetheless wept with the bitterest tears.
        Hear our supplication

and spare us such wrath as divinity sometimes
        can visit on mortals.

SECOND CHORISTER: The helpless subjects of kings, we are
        helpless
                toys of the gods:
        the best way is to keep quiet,
                avoiding their notice,   390
        but on occasions when history's quirk may
                invite their attention,
        we hope to be pleasing, framing our chorus
                of praises and thanks.
        Jupiter, ruler of thunder and lightning,
                catastrophe's keeper,
        into your care we commend ourselves, hoping
                to find the forbearance
        a father would show to his unruly children,
                or even some fondness.   400

FIRST CHORISTER: Accept our professions of reverence and terror
                in varied proportions,
        and do not despise us. Being your creatures,
                we are as you made us
        and do what we can in a short span of time as
                we try to acknowledge
        the world that you gave us, both splendid and dreadful,
                and all that there is . . .

SECOND CHORISTER: But look, a soldier comes, and with good
        tidings,
        for the martial spear he carries is wreathed in laurel.   410
        I recognize the man: it is Eurybates,
        the king's herald.

(EURYBATES enters)

FIRST CHORISTER: We bid you welcome, sir.

EURYBATES: Praise the gods! I rejoice to gaze again
  on the holy shrines of the deities of this house.
  Their long years of wandering ended, the weary
  men come home at last, and I, among them.
  Scarcely do I trust my brimming eyes.
  (*Addressing the people*)
  Revere the mighty gods and offer thanks
  for what they have allowed to happen—the glory
  of Agamemnon. Victor of the war,
  he returns at last to his own land and house!   420

(CLYTEMNESTRA *enters, having heard the last of* EURYBATES' *words*)

CLYTEMNESTRA: Wonderful news is this, and blessed. I thank
    you!
  But where is he now? At sea? Ashore? After years,
  these last moments of waiting are hardest to bear.

EURYBATES: He is safe, has landed, and comes now from the
    harbor
  while guards try to restrain the cheering crowds.

CLYTEMNESTRA: We thank those gods to whom we have long
    prayed.
  But tell me, is Menelaus well? And my sister?

EURYBATES: I hope they are, but cannot say for certain.
  The seas and winds were capricious; our fleet was scattered;
  in the heavy storms one could not see from the deck   430
  of one to the mast and reefed sails of another.
  Agamemnon lost more of his men on the voyage
  than during all those years we spent at Troy.

CLYTEMNESTRA: Tell what happened. Say it, however bad.

EURYBATES: A bitter tale of woe shot through with gladness.

CLYTEMNESTRA: In suspense, we imagine the worst. Speak, sir,
    at once.

EURYBATES: In haste, we went to sea, and learned again
    to walk without the drag of a sword belt.
    Our shields were piled at the stern, and, honest men
    of peaceful times, we worked at the oars. The king's   440
    vessel led the way, its golden prow
    gleaming in the sun. The trumpet blast
    signaled the rowers' beat, as a thousand ships
    filed out of the harbor, filled their sails,
    and moved in triumphal parade across the water's
    sunlit dazzle. A splendid sight, and behind us,
    the last glimpse of the wreck of Troy. Who
    can forget that awesome moment? Strong young men
    pulled at the oars in rhythmic swings, and foam
    hissed under gunwales and purled in a wake of diamonds.   450
    The wind from the east picked up, and the men could rest
    at least for a time as it carried us offshore
    and speak once more, before they escaped from us
    to fly on anyone's breath as commonplaces,
    of those things we had seen with our own eyes—
    Hector's threats, and then his broken body
    dragging along in the dust outside the walls;
    Priam coming to ransom the bloody meat
    that was his son; and then, on the altar, Priam's
    own blood. Who could credit such tales   460
    as dolphins played in the sunlit water around us?
    Behind us, Ida was only a blurry shape,
    and then it disappeared as the light gave way
    in a sunset where a lone gray cloud extended
    across the western sky. The stars came out,
    twinkling in gentle winds, and fresher,
    as the sails slapped and bellied and waves came up,
    and salt spray stung. The stars abandoned the sky
    that moaned now with a steadily rising wind,
    and then the storm broke and bounced us around   470
    like a child's plaything of North Wind and of West.

Rain pelted the open boats, and spray
rose up to argue, salt against sweet water,
but all of it cold and boding us no good.
    There is no sea below or sky above,
but the two realms merging together, as day
and night are confused, with all foundation gone.
The Styx cannot be worse, for the darkness shines
in sudden jabs of lightning to let us see
our comrades' terror-stricken faces or, worse,   480
empty benches where comrades have just now
huddled but were swept away, all brave,
battle-hardened men, and our good friends,
suddenly gone. The rest of us behaved
badly, I fear, confusion if not panic
preventing any concerted, sensible action.
Who knows if there was a way we might have saved
some of our number? What hurt us most was to watch
the ships ram one another, the crashing prows
staving in vessels to left and right. To cries   490
for help, our helmsmen tried to respond but met
destruction instead as wild waves flung us about,
and timbers crashed as if with the sounds of battle.
Some of the vessels swamped, and some turned over,
their keels riding the turbulent water with men
trapped inside and no way for us to reach them.
Our oars snapped, turned into spears, impaled
a few who flailed in the water, fighting for breath.
Despair came over us all and a kind of calm,
for nothing was human now. It was out of our hands,   500
with reason, bravery, all experience useless.
Horror froze our limbs; in shock the sailors
turned to prayer for help, for mercy, or merely
an end to the torment. What the Trojans felt those last
terrible days, we felt—that bitter taste
of fear, part bile and blood, and part hot tears.
We envied the Trojans now for they were past it,
had gone through their ordeal to that release
we suppose that death must bring. So Agamemnon

thought of Priam; Pyrrhus thought of his father,   510
Achilles; Ulysses remembered the mighty Ajax.
Where was the good of victory now, or survival?
What was the point of all our efforts, if now
the living envied the dead? And where is there justice,
if fishermen and traders ply the sea
in relative safety, while we, the heroes of Troy,
as if of no account, could be tossed away
by unthinking walls of water and mindless winds?
Virtue and villainy, equals? Bravery useless?
To hold onto life emptied of meaning is stupid,   520
a matter of habit or mere animal instinct.
Pushed to beyond what men should have to bear,
we turned our wet faces up to heaven,
or what we supposed in that heaving maelstrom was up.
We prayed to the gods, or rebuked, or even defied them,
daring them at last to explain themselves,
but meaning itself was mocked. Assume the worst,
that the gods were now imposing on us this penance
for having conquered Troy. . . . But Trojans were with us,
whatever was left of their number, slaves and captives,   530
but still Trojans.
                    These were our frantic thoughts,
but not a word was said or, if there was,
the wind ripped it away, tearing our breath
as it had torn our sails and spars and hulls
to useless fragments. Lightning flashed to show us
how abject we were and helpless: the ghastly stabs
of light came as shocks, wounds to the spirit
and body, too. Minerva borrowed her father's
terrible weapons to hurl down. Little Ajax
was shortening sail, the halyard clenched in his teeth,   540
when one bolt hit, grazed him, knocked him down,
dazed him, so that he was pitched overboard
with the next wave. It would have been enough
to kill a lesser man, but, like a rock
on which the waters crash but uselessly,
he broke through to the surface, water streaming

in rivers down his face. Somehow, he'd found
a foothold there on a nearly submerged rock,
and set himself upon it, grabbed the ship,
and held on, straining with all his strength, and yelled   550
insane defiance: "No! Fire and water,
earth and air! Hear me! I am Ajax.
Hector, I fought, and Mars himself, and survived.
And do you suppose that you can bring me down,
cruel goddess? Even your father's lightning
I have withstood . . ."
                              But then the rock gave way
on which he stood, and mighty Ajax lurched,
toppled, lost his handhold on the gunwale,
and disappeared.
                              Who could bear such a loss
and yet have the wit to wonder how he stood   560
on a rock that way? We had been blown off course,
had strayed away from the channel, and new perils
came to assail us—shallows and hidden rocks
onto which ships crashed, and broke, and foundered,
wallowing helplessly, hitting their sister ships
in the great armada. The sea had done its worst,
and now the land we'd hoped to reach joined in
to do us mischief also.
                              But then a light,
a beacon, showed us where to go: we struggled
with what strength we had left to make that passage   570
to what we believed was safety. Palamedes'
angry father, Nauplius, was waiting,
having brooded all those years on his revenge
for what we'd done to his son. The beacons were his,
snares, hung in the trees above the rocks.
Too late we heard the timbers break and cries
of hurt and drowning men. Those who survived
could see at dawn the carnage from which, even now,
a few are coming with heavy heart from the harbor.

CLYTEMNESTRA: I am glad my lord is safe but grieve to hear   580
   of this new loss we have had to suffer. Gods!
   When will you relent? Let us give thanks
   for those who have been spared. Let flowers be brought
   in wreaths of celebration, and let the flutes
   intone their sacred music as beasts are led
   to the holy altars for solemn sacrifice.
      But look what comes! A train of mourning women,
   their hair unbound. The Trojan captives, I think.
   The proud one in the lead must be Cassandra.

(CHORUS *of Trojan women enters, with* CASSANDRA *leading*)

FIRST CHORISTER: The way is clear, and the gate, open,   590
   an escape that invites the proud soul,
   but the body hesitates at the threshold,
   and will not step over.

SECOND CHORISTER: We are not afraid. Or say that we fear
   even more the dreadful prospect
   each additional hour brings
   of some new outrage.

FIRST CHORISTER: Instead, we retain a sentimental
   fondness for this worthless package
   we confuse with ourselves, the poor body   600
   the lungs and heart,

   muddling on, as if nothing had happened,
   and going about their repetitive business.
   Served with the bitter portion of exile,
   it chews and it swallows.

SECOND CHORISTER: At the storm's worst, we clung to the vessel
   as if for dear life, as if our lives were
   dear. The waters were offering freedom,
   but who could let go

and simply relax for a moment her grip   610
on a terrible present and shameful future?
The mind and soul can suggest what they like,
but the body balks.

FIRST CHORISTER: We who lived through the fall of Troy
should know how to hate the eyes and ears
that brought the terrible news our brains
could not accept.

The piteous cries of the dying, the fires,
the sobbing of widows and wails of the children
were no more persuasive than vivid nightmares   620
from which we might wake.

SECOND CHORISTER: Who can imagine, having seen it,
a votive horse at the gate of the city,
and our own children grabbing the ropes
to pull it inside?

Who can bear to recall the rejoicing
of parents relieved that their children were spared?
The shrines of the gods were covered with flowers.
Our tears were of joy.

FIRST CHORISTER: That day, Priam and Hecuba, happy   630
for the first time since Hector had fallen,
led the thanksgiving. We were sure that the city
was spared, and the walls

the gods themselves had built would endure.
How could we know they were already toppled
and Priam was all but stretched out on the altar
where Pyrrhus would kill him?

SECOND CHORISTER: I saw with my own eyes how the sword
   glinted and fell. There was not much blood—
   the sword was so sharp, or he was so old.   640
   The flood was of tears

   from us who were witnesses, rubbing our eyes
   as if to erase that unbearable sight
   that remains still as an afterimage
   wherever we look.

FIRST CHORISTER: What can men and women endure?
   There ought to be limits. A heart should break
   but doesn't, keeps on with its idiot beating,
   and adds to the torture.

   Weeping and howling, we vent our hurt   650
   and also outrage at what the gods,
   pitiless, lofty, do to torment us
   innocent mortals.

CHORUS: Let us mourn together for Priam,
   the frail old man whom Pyrrhus dispatched
   inside the temple at Jupiter's altar,
   there, where he prayed . . .

CASSANDRA: Leave the mourning for Priam to me, his daughter.
   You have enough of your own dead to weep for.
   Losses cannot be shared. One weeps alone,   660
   however many acquaintances presume
   to intrude on one's grief. . . . What do they know about it
   whose empty condolences cut like little knives?

FIRST CHORISTER: Solitude is a bruise. To mix
   the tears of grief is a kind of healing.
   Strong as you are, do not despise
   your friends, who understand you better
   than strangers can. We must mourn together,
   as all the birds in the forest join in

with Philomel's sad song, and Procne's,   670
and the whole wood, the whole world
takes up the dirge. We, too, are distracted,
almost maddened, by pain and know
its terrible truth. We exclude all else
as invidious delusion and lies.

SECOND CHORISTER: There is no measure for our weeping;
it cannot enlarge, cannot diminish.
All the moans that have ever been ripped
from stricken mothers, daughters, or wives
will therefore neither add nor detract   680
from our absolute agony here.

FIRST CHORISTER: For your own sake, do not despise us.
Do not reject our harmonizing
with your cry. We may not help you,
but neither can we help but weep
as we wait for time to numb the pain
if not one way, then another,
for flesh either learns to endure or dies.

SECOND CHORISTER: Lady, it hurts us to see you struggle,
to watch as you tear the holy fillets   690
out of your hair. The gods may yet
attend somehow to our eloquent need.
Calm yourself, and show them respect.

CASSANDRA: What can the gods do to me now? What further
hurt could they contrive? All history
has come to an end and, careless, I defy
the deities in charge of it. What father,
what sister can they take from me? Their altars
are sated with the lifeblood of my house.
The corpses in tombs must mourn for one another.   700
No one is left alive to pay them homage
or offer the bare respect of a spray of flowers. . . .
Every woman who walked those royal halls,

excepting only Helen, is widowed, enslaved,
or driven mad. Outside the ruined walls
of what was a proud city, Hecuba, noble,
a queen, crawls on the ground, howls like a dog,
and, having rejected reason, despises speech.

FIRST CHORISTER: In time to come, who will credit
    what we see here? How do we bear   710
    to watch the princess, bride of Apollo,
    cursing the gods, rejecting their gifts
    of understanding, light, and life?
    A beautiful woman, she has been hurt,
    sickened, her mind is pushed to its limit.
    See how her lips tremble, how pale
    and haggard her face. . . . Her heart, cornered,
    fights as a trapped animal might,
    in spite of the odds, against the gods.

CASSANDRA: O Apollo, why have you forsaken   720
    that girl you loved? No longer am I yours.
    My only prayer now is to be let free.
    Take from me the terrible gift. There is no
    reason for it, or purpose. I cannot turn back
    the hours and days and warn that thus and thus
    must you do, or else. . . . The worst has happened. The end
    has come, is past. I wander the earth and rave
    truths nobody cares about, give answers
    to questions no one has asked. I rub my eyes
    with helpless fists that can never wipe away   730
    the vision of Ida, a shepherd boy, his flock,
    and three goddesses, toying with one another,
    him, and all the world, and know no more
    than he did then—except for the pain, the bleeding,
    the echoing clang of metal on metal, the moans
    of the dying, and longer moans of those who lived.
       Visions come to me still, but to no purpose.
    I do not care, don't want to know, don't want
    to tell them, warn those people whom I hate. . . .

I delight now in the misery of the world   740
that only confirms my own. Who is this monster,
the issue of incest that comes to do grave mischief?
Who is the woman, maddened, a bloodied ax
waving about her head? A lion comes,
king of the beasts, home from the hunt to find
cold welcome, lies in a river of his own blood,
gnawed by the lioness there. Do I believe this?
Will what I say make it better or worse? Should death
come in surprise or greet them, wave from afar,
make itself known, and advance with heavy step   750
a horrible hand held out from which there is no
evasion or escape? I feel on my cheeks
still burning paths of the tears from terrible visions
that were not dreams but happened, stained the daylight,
offending the sight of the sun itself. My father's
poor body, lifeless, stretched on the altar;
my brother Hector's body, dragged in the dirt;
my brother Troilus dead; and Deiphobus
dead. They have all crossed to the other world,
while I still tarry here, and can't think why.   760
(*Intoning and dancing*)

The mad Fates, cruel sisters,
dancing among the shades of hell,
wave their whips and kick the bones
of the rotting corpses. This they love,
to see what our pretensions come to,
and watch shades that suffer still,
all life gone excepting pain.
See how Tantalus, hungry, thirsty,
forgets himself and covers his eyes
but cannot blot the dreadful vision   770
of what is to come to his hateful house.
They know what I know. I know what they know.
How does one bear to see it, live through it
once, then see it again, and again?

(She collapses)

SECOND CHORISTER: Her frenzy has spent itself at last. She falls.

FIRST CHORISTER: A terrible thing. I have sometimes been in the
     temple
and watched as the priest missed his aim and the bull
staggered, swayed, hung there a moment, stricken,
before he collapsed. Come, let us lift her up.

(They try to do so but cannot)

SECOND CHORISTER: But look, crowned with laurel,
     Agamemnon   780
returns to his city.

FIRST CHORISTER: Clytemnestra greets him.
     Together they walk, arm in arm, through the gate.

(AGAMEMNON *and* CLYTEMNESTRA *enter. She goes into the palace;*
he remains.)

AGAMEMNON: *(Delivering what is clearly a prepared speech)*
     At last I return to my father's house and safety.
     I thank the gods, and weep in joy to see
     these walls, these hills, this earth—to which all Asia
     has given with heaven's help her exotic spoils.
     (Noticing CASSANDRA, *he interrupts himself)*
     But who is this priestess? What has happened. Help her!
     Quickly, some water. Yes, yes, she revives . . .
     (He recognizes her)
     Oh, it's you. There's nothing for you to fear.
     Get up. We are safe at home. It's a celebration.   790
     Our woes are behind us now.

CASSANDRA: So you said at Troy.

AGAMEMNON: Let us kneel down and pray.

CASSANDRA: As my father
                                                                      prayed
  when Pyrrhus killed him?

AGAMEMNON: In the name of almighty Jove!

CASSANDRA: Jove's altar it was, as you surely remember!

AGAMEMNON: This isn't Troy, woman!

CASSANDRA: I know, too well.

AGAMEMNON: There is nothing further to fear. We are now at
  home.

CASSANDRA: Wherever there is a Helen, there is a Troy.

AGAMEMNON: Watch your tongue. Remember, you are a slave.

CASSANDRA: My freedom is close at hand—death's
  manumission.

AGAMEMNON: You have no cause to fear.

CASSANDRA: But you have
                                                                      much.   800

AGAMEMNON: What can a conqueror fear?

CASSANDRA: What he does not.

AGAMEMNON: (*to his* ATTENDANTS)
  Take her away. Restrain her. She'll calm down.
  She doesn't know what she's saying, cannot help
  these ravings. . . . She had the gift of prophecy once,
  but now that Troy is fallen, she's merely mad.
  Sad, but there it is. I go to give thanks
  for my return from the wars. The gods are kind!

(ATTENDANTS *take* CASSANDRA *away.* AGAMEMNON *exits into the palace.*)

CHORUS: What a man does, that man is.
    Whatever he achieves or wins,
    or makes with his hands, that is his nature,   810
    that is his being—what his name means.

    Some deeds remain in the minds of men
    and are passed about from hearer to hearer,
    all of whom take comfort or courage
    from knowing what one of our kind has done.

    The deed is not diminished but lives
    stronger with every telling. The hero
    of whom they speak is elevated,
    no longer mere mortal but godly.

FIRST CHORISTER: If one man makes that leap, we all   820
    can aim higher, or only dream.
    All were ennobled when Hercules
    married our world to that of Olympus.

    By dint of his strength and courage, you
    and I are different from what we were,
    must aspire to better, and blame ourselves
    all the more for our woeful failures.

SECOND CHORISTER: What Hercules did once, Agamemnon
    recalls and even seems to rival:
    setting out from Argos to Asia,   830
    leader of mighty heroes, destroyer

    of one of the world's great cities. His name
    will be in the mouths of men forever;
    of his great deeds will the poets sing
    as we recite those of Hercules.

FIRST CHORISTER: The world stood still at his begetting,
    and seems yet to have stopped—his triumphs
    can never fade: we tell the stories
    as if we had seen them happen ourselves.

    The powerful Nemean lion, he crushed   840
    and the Erymathian boar that had ravaged
    Arcadian fields, and the bull of Crete.
    The Hydra with many heads, he slew. . . .

    His was an arm like any arm
    of flesh and sinew and bone but stronger;
    his fist was like any mortal fist,
    but see what it did, what it could do.

SECOND CHORISTER: The triple-monster Geryon
    he vanquished with his crashing club;
    the Thracian herd of horrific horses   850
    Diomedes had trained, he mastered,

    turning that tyrant into the gory
    fodder his horses had learnt to prefer
    to the mash that nourishes their kind.
    Every one of these deeds was a marvel.

FIRST CHORISTER: All together, they beggar belief,
    and change for the rest of time the standard
    of what the measure of man must be.
    What other mortal dared descend

    to the underworld and drag the dog   860
    by its triple lead to light that dazzled
    even Cerberus silent? But he
    accomplished whatever the Fates proposed.

SECOND CHORISTER: And Hercules' arrows, in Philoctetes'
   hands, at last brought the city down.
   Among the host Agamemnon led,
   one may then reckon Hercules too . . .

(A *shriek is heard. Then* CASSANDRA *enters and addresses the audience.*)

CASSANDRA: A wonder! A marvel! After ten long years,
   the moment at last arrives. I do not dream,
   but see what all Troy dreamt in that long night   870
   come true. In ruins now, Troy rises up
   rejoicing; ghosts are dancing now, triumphant
   in a great reversal! Priam's bloody corpse
   performs a jig at Agamemnon's fall.
   I have learned to hate my gift, but second sight
   is precious now. I see it about to happen,
   and see it happen! All the pains of my life
   have turned to pleasures, ecstasies now, in this
   grand moment. I feast upon their feast!
   I see the banquet table's purple couches,   880
   the golden cups refilled with the wine from the golden
   vessels of Assaracus—my great-grandfather!
   And there he is, the king, at the head of the table,
   on the highest couch, in the gaudiest robes. He lolls
   in all his stolen finery, but his wife
   holds out to him a robe she has made herself
   of cloth she has woven with her own hand, and bids him
   put it on. My soul trembles to see
   so fine a moment. Can such treachery come
   to Agamemnon, the proud? Aegisthus watches   890
   his paramour as she holds out this destruction
   to the cuckold husband he desires dead.
   Agamemnon puts the robe on, and the smile
   he wears on his face contorts as the understanding
   blooms too late in his mind that he is undone.
   The meshes tighten, bind his limbs, disable
   all resistance. Snared, netted, trapped,

he is enshrouded. Aegisthus makes the first,
almost playful cut. And then another.
In the woods, wild boars, enraged, will struggle   900
but only tighten their bonds. Like them, he writhes
in vain, as Aegisthus cuts again, again,
again. And now she comes with the double ax,
raises it up, oh yes, and brings it down
with a great whack, and the head is almost off
but hangs by a precarious thread of skin.
And now he comes again, and hacks at the corpse:
Thyestes' son and Helen's sister together
are doing what Greeks do. Agamemnon's life
and mine are both complete now and fulfilled.   910

(*She turns to see* ELECTRA *enter leading her young brother,*
ORESTES)

ELECTRA: Flee while you can. Run! You are the last
  hope of this house. Escape the criminals. Hide
  wherever you can. But hurry. The time is short.
  (*She sees an approaching chariot*)
  Who comes there? A stranger, driving his horses
  fast. . . . A friend? Can we trust him? We've no choice . . .
  (ORESTES *tries to hide behind* ELECTRA)
  No, dear brother. You must not fear the stranger.
  In our house, it's the relatives one fears.
  Be bold, brother, as princes should always be.

(STROPHIUS *enters in a chariot, accompanied by his young son,*
PYLADES)

STROPHIUS: Children, do you know me? I am your uncle,
  Strophius, king of Phocis. Don't be afraid.   920
  I am here to pay my respects to Agamemnon,
  home from the wars. Why do you weep? Your father
  is well, I trust? What cause have you for grief
  and, if I am not mistaken, terror?
  Speak up. Whatever has happened, I am your friend!

ELECTRA: My father has just been murdered. Mother killed him,
    and now she seeks to kill my little brother.
    Aegisthus, mother's lover, rules Mycenæ.

STROPHIUS: This is his celebration? This was his triumph?

ELECTRA: In memory of my father, I beg you, Uncle,   930
    take Orestes. My mother and her lover
    mean him harm. The gods are cruel to this house.
    We despair of kindness from any quarter.

STROPHIUS: A desperate lot this is. Agamemnon's death
    frightens us all. No one is safe, no one
    can rest easy, now or ever. But yes,
    I'll take Orestes and hide him, danger or no.
    In its face, one must try to behave well.
    Good fortune invites friendship, while ill luck
    demands it. Come, then, son. Come here. Get up!   940
    (ORESTES *mounts into the chariot*)
    Take this wreath of olive branches, prize
    of victory in games, and put it on.
    And take this sacred palm branch. Hold it up
    to cover your face. Stay next to Pylades.
    Stand up straight, holding your head up high,
    and look as if you belong here. No one will dare
    question who you are. Now, let us take leave
    of the worst place in Greece and all the world.

(*They drive off in the chariot, leaving* ELECTRA *behind*)

ELECTRA: They are gone.
                         If he is safe, it does not matter
    what happens to me: life or death.   950
    I don't know which is worse now, do not care . . .
    (*She sees* CLYTEMNESTRA *approaching*)
    My mother comes, her hands still red with the gore
    of Father's corpse.

(*To* CASSANDRA, *who has been observing all this*)
Take me to the altar.
Together, we will seek what protection it offers.

CLYTEMNESTRA: Wicked child! What are you doing here?
A virgin, walking the public streets? It's shameless!

ELECTRA: A virgin, I flee our house of shame and sin.

CLYTEMNESTRA: Whatever your claim, nobody will believe it!

ELECTRA: Of course not. I am your daughter, after all.

CLYTEMNESTRA: Watch what you say!

ELECTRA: You instruct me in
   manners now?   960

CLYTEMNESTRA: Insolent miss, I can also instruct you in pain.

ELECTRA: I admit you're good at that—grand mistress, even!

CLYTEMNESTRA: A big mouth on a small child. We're afraid!

ELECTRA: But who is "we"? Your lord, Agamemnon, is dead!
   Is the mourning done? Are you so soon remarried?

CLYTEMNESTRA: All you need know is that I am still the queen,
   and you must obey me. Where's your little brother?

ELECTRA: Far from Mycenae.

CLYTEMNESTRA: Tell me where he has gone!

ELECTRA· And will you tell me where my father has gone?

CLYTEMNESTRA: Stop playing games.

ELECTRA: He's playing hide-and-
                                                seek.   970
You're "it," and he is safe. Which should be enough
for a loving mother.

CLYTEMNESTRA: But not for an angry one.
Today, you die!

ELECTRA: By your encrimsoned hand?
I do hope so! I'll leave this sacred altar
gladly, to join my father. Will you stab me
with a dagger in the back? Or use the ax
to cut my head off? Or slit my throat? Your already
bloody hand will need to be washed but once.

(AEGISTHUS *enters*)

CLYTEMNESTRA: Aegisthus, help me. This insulting child
refuses to tell me where her brother is hidden.   980

AEGISTHUS: Young lady, I advise you to obey.
Behave yourself. Do not defy your mother.

ELECTRA: You? Give lessons in conduct? You, the monster,
your sister's son, your father's own grandson,
adulterer, killer, offer me advice?

CLYTEMNESTRA: Why do you hesitate? Aegisthus, kill her!
Cut off her damned head. I will not stop you.

AEGISTHUS: Better keep her alive down in a dungeon,
beaten, starving, thirsty, covered in filth,
and always able to end her pain by speaking   990
the words we wait to hear—where is the brother?
We'll drag her blinking into the light, and she
will beg to speak. And then beg us to kill her.

ELECTRA: Let me die now!

AEGISTHUS: That would be pointlessly kind.

ELECTRA: What can be worse than death?

AEGISTHUS: As you will learn:
    life, when you wish to die. Everyone dies
    sooner or later. And you shall come to envy
    those who have been released from their trials. Guards,
    take her away, down to the darkest dungeon,
    where she may lie in chains and discover that stone   1000
    walls are as hard as the will of any girl.

CLYTEMNESTRA: (*Indicating* CASSANDRA)
    But she can die right now, that captive bride,
    mistress of the late king. Do it at once,
    that she may follow him whose prize she was.

CASSANDRA: Of my own free will, I go, glad to deliver
    the news those Trojan heroes yearn to hear
    of a ruin worse than Troy's, and more disgraceful—
    Agamemnon, slain by a faithless wife.
    The life I hated, having survived the fall
    of my great city, you have made sweet again.   1010
    I thank you, madam.

CLYTEMNESTRA: Pay her no mind. She's mad.
    Put her out of her misery.

CASSANDRA: Your madness
    is yet to come.
    (*Staring into space and smiling*)
                        But it comes! I see it already.

(*Laughs, and is led away as the curtain falls*)